CREATING IMPACT

CHANGEMAKERS WHO OVERCAME ADVERSITY TO CREATE A POSITIVE IMPACT IN THE WORLD

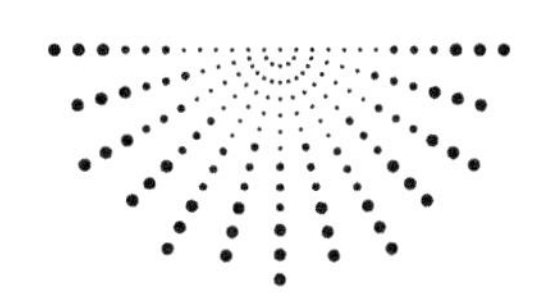

DINA BEHRMAN SAMI WUNDER
MELANIE MACINTYRE CASSIE MORRIS-DALTON
LEIGH DANIEL LIBBY PARKER HEATHER STEWART
BRIGID HOLDER CANDICE COLGAN
ANDREW COWIE JENNY VUKOVCAN
STACY ANN BRYAN EVA GRUBER JOANNE MARTIN
MILDA SABIENE DR. KRISTINA TICKLER WELSOME
MARIA FONTANA

INSPIRED WORLD PUBSLIHING

CONTENTS

INTRODUCTION

As a journalist I was always taught to look for the 'triumph over adversity' story arc. Because we all face adversity and challenges in our lives, so stories from people who have not only overcome difficult times but have come out the other side even stronger have a truly universal appeal.

I have always appreciated people who aren't afraid to speak out about challenges they've been through, because there is always something for us to learn from them. Whether or not we've been through the same challenge or something similar, we've all had to face difficulties of some kind, be that in relation to our health, our work, our relationships or something else. And hearing people's stories of resilience, of succeeding against the odds, of not giving up, is endlessly inspiring.

"Creating Impact: Changemakers Who Overcame Adversity To Create A Positive Impact In The World", includes stories from 17 leading entrepreneurs and business leaders from across the globe who have overcome challenges from depression, trauma, bereavement, and illness, to heartbreak, anxiety, job loss, burnout and Imposter Syndrome, but have come out the other side and are now making a positive impact in the world with the work they do.

Each chapter shares a unique story from someone who has triumphed over adversity and shows us that even when things look tough, there is always light at the end of the tunnel and that good things can grow from difficult circumstances.

Some of the subjects covered are light-hearted and some include sensitive topics, but they all ultimately offer the reader the same message: that whatever the challenge, humans are resilient and there is always hope.

The book is full of motivating and uplifting stories from a diverse range of voices, and it's our intention that you will gain inspiration, insight and wisdom from them.

I am so inspired by all of the authors in this book who are individually and collectively making a hugely positive impact in the world with the work they do. I hope you enjoy reading their stories and take what you need from them.

Dina Behrman
Inspired World Publishing

1

SAMI WUNDER

FROM HEARTBROKEN TO A MULTI-MILLION DOLLAR LOVE COACHING EMPIRE

"*Sorry, Sami. You are a wonderful woman, but I cannot give you what you want. I am not feeling it for you.*"

I remember those words falling on me with the weight of a thousand bricks.

I felt like I couldn't breathe. I felt humiliated, ashamed, and heartbroken.

I sat in my one-bedroom apartment in Berlin that night and bawled my eyes out to my sister.

"Is something wrong with me?" I remember asking her, as she passionately denied agreeing with me.

It was as though my greatest nightmare was coming true.

The man I thought was 'the one' for me was suddenly walking out on me after two months of intense dating. I thought our connection was the best I had ever shared with a man. I was even seeing a future for us together, talking about babies and marriage and yet here I was. Again.

Intelligent, good looking, hard-working and perpetually single!

To tell you the truth, I felt so disillusioned that night that I was close to giving up on this whole thing called love.

I was also dangerously close to giving up on believing in men and their goodness. In fact, a part of me even wondered if all of this struggle for love was worth it. Wouldn't it be easier to continue focusing on my career success and win on that front in life instead of constantly facing rejection in love?

At least I felt I had some control over my career success but when it came to men and love, I felt utterly helpless.

There was pain and there was disillusionment, so imagine my surprise when I heard a calm, almost wise voice inside me whisper – '*Don't give up. Not just yet. You are going to be a wife and a mother one day. It's what you want and you must keep that desire for love alive in your heart. This pain has a bigger purpose.*'

Those words soothed my soul, bringing me an instant sense of much needed relief.

Exhausted from my heavy emotions, I finally fell asleep at 3 am that night, holding close to my heart the words – '*This pain has a bigger purpose.*'

When I woke up the next morning, I was still sad but something inside me had shifted. I felt the strength within me return. The words, '*There is a bigger purpose to this pain*', kept echoing in my ears with a ferocity I had never felt before.

I experienced a kind of clarity in the moment that was refreshing, given how confused I had felt before. Somehow, I just knew that my next step was to figure out where I was going wrong with men in my romantic relationships. I knew that figuring this out was going to be significant in my life, without knowing how. I felt it in my bones that there was something big waiting to reveal itself to me.

On the personal front too, I knew I didn't want to keep going this way. My dream of marriage and kids was important to me, a non-negotiable. And so, I decided to take my love life into my own hands vs. relying on God, fate or the Universe to make my dreams come true.

Also, as a consistently A grade student, with gold medals in Economics from Delhi University and a full scholarship from the German Government to pursue my Masters in Public Policy in Berlin, I was smart enough to know that it was insane to keep doing the same things with men and expect different results. I was ready to try different things, mindsets, and behaviours now, to get the results I wanted in my love life.

And so I charted forward, even in the midst of this acute adversity and pain.

I downloaded dozens of books on healthy romantic relationships from the internet's top relationship experts back then and consumed them in a matter of a few weeks.

What I learnt in those weeks changed my life.

It would not be an exaggeration to say that a new version of the woman I was meant to be was born.

I am aware that at first sight, when you look at dating and relationship advice on the internet, it can be really superficial. Many male gurus teach women two hundred ways to text a man and five hundred ways to seduce him.

However, if you dig in deeper, the subject of healing your love life and romantic relationships is the greatest journey of inner transformation one can ever take. Our intimate relationships, after all, are the greatest mirror to our own inner world and what we believe we deserve.

As Stephen Chboky rightly says, - *"We accept the love we think we deserve."*

Given what I was learning about my sense of self-worth - having a strong sense of personal boundaries, how I was acting in my masculine energy around men vs. embracing my vulnerability and feminine energy around them - the pain and adversity I had to go through to become this woman was already starting to feel worth it.

Within months, I was dating several high-quality men who were vying for my time and attention. My single girlfriends and colleagues from work could hardly believe the transformation that was happening inside of me while they were still struggling.

I attracted, met and got engaged to my amazing husband Christopher within nine months of meeting him and my life changed for the good, forever.

The pieces of my life were coming together, and it was all making sense.

Who knew back then that the pain from that night would be the one thing that propels me to prioritise my love life and help me attract my most amazing husband?

Who knew back then that that pain would go onto metamorphose into my greatest gift and life purpose in this lifetime?

That I will go on to become a leading international love coach for high achieving women in the years to come and impact thousands and thousands of lives positively on this planet?

That I would run a multi-million-dollar company that helps other successful women find and keep amazing love?

That my work would go on to get featured in Forbes Magazine, Time magazine and the BBC and Business Insider would hail me as the 'Relationship Guru' for modern, highly achieving women who want to attract and maintain amazing relationships and marriages.

Today, as a happily married wife of over eight years and a mother of two beautiful boys that keep me on my toes, I am so glad that I did not succumb to my pain that night.

Not only for myself, but also for my clients, my community, the women who look up to me and the women I am meant to serve.

I shudder to think that had I given up that night, a lot of the magic that exists in my life today would not be there. My adoring husband Chris, my two beautiful children, my work that brings me so much fame and good will and blessings from my clients, none of this would have come to fruition had I given up on my desire for love that night.

I am glad that I did not let adversity win over me that night and at the same time I am grateful to the Universe for putting me through that pain. Without it, I wouldn't have learnt what I needed to learn to realise my full potential in life. And in love.

In fact, it is my hot, passionate belief that it is exactly that adversity that catapulted me to the next level in my life and love and took me from being single and struggling to be happily married and adored. From working for other people's dreams to creating a life of freedom where I get to design my own schedule and serve dream clients that include celebrities, TV stars, professional career women and many more.

Below I would like to share with you what I know to be true about adversity, after having built my successful company, making many bold choices in business and love and having helped over 300 of my clients walk down the aisle.

1. Do not let adversity intimidate you

I have come to find that adversity is like a bully. If you let it bring you down and intimidate you, it enjoys your reaction and serves you more of the same pain. However, if you look it in the eye and remind yourself that you are stronger than what is happening to you, soon the same bully starts to feel smaller before you and loses its desire to hurt you. After all, you are not giving it the reaction of sadness and turmoil it wants from you.

When I share this, I am reminded of another time in my life, where things felt really difficult. I had sorted my own love life by this time, but I was still missing that feeling of creating a true impact in the lives of others.

In late 2014, Chris and I moved to Paris as a married couple because of his new job in the Aerospace sector. During this time, there was a transition phase of a few months where I found it hard to find a job locally, because I could not speak French. I was still doing consultancy contracts for some top international development organisations but my heart craved more meaningful and direct impact. I wanted to help people, do something great in the world and there was a fire in my belly that I wanted to express but I just did not know how to do it.

This was yet another time in my life when I felt adversity was momentarily winning and I was losing.

I had so much turmoil coming up inside me. I felt disconnected with my magic and my own power to steer my life.

I remember bursting out into tears in a desperate moment one evening, while waiting for Chris to return from work for dinner together. Instead of welcoming him home, after a long day of work, I dumped him on several existential questions-

- Why was I sitting at home after being a gold medalist Economist?
- What was I going to do with my brains and intelligence now?
- This wasn't the life I had in mind for myself and what am I supposed to do now?

Thankfully, I had a loving man by my side who held me and reminded me – *"I understand this is hard but something big is coming to you through this phase. Dońt let it bring you down.Dońt let adversity win."*

2. Trust That Something Big Is Trying to Come Through When Things Feel Hard

That moment was like serendipity.

I was stunned when Chris used words similar to the voice that I had heard in my apartment that night in Berlin, when I was in pain after my heartbreak.

"Something big is coming to you through this phase," - Wow!

He said this even though I had never shared with him the words of that voice. There was no reason to.

Somehow those words soothed my soul once again and I decided to trust the process.

I literally told adversity, *'Screw you - I am bigger than this!'* and decided to actively enjoy my free time in Paris, trusting that the 'big thing' that needed to be revealed would find its way to me, at the right time.

Over the next few weeks, I decided to simply enjoy this phase of my life in Paris, one of the most beautiful cities in the world. We visited Disneyland Paris, saw a cabaret show at the Moulin Rouge and went on day trips to the Palace of Versailles. Those were some of the best weeks of my life.

My dreams were nowhere close to coming true, but I had decided not to let adversity bully me. I had decided to choose my own happiness and place trust in the big plan that I knew was going to be revealed.

3. Pay attention to the signs when they come

Whether you are looking to start your own business, take your business to the next level, scale up to six or seven figures or create more impact in the world through your gifts, there's going to be adversity on the way and there is going to be signs and support from the Universe.

In my experience, you have to be excited to find the signs and receive them when they are given to you.

How magical was it then that one day when sitting in a Parisian Cafe and scrolling through Facebook, I saw an advertisement on getting trained as a coach. They said I could do it from home and help people. Something about that idea really stuck with me.

I went home with my heart pulsating with excitement. Sitting with Chris, I remember saying - "What is the one thing that I know I can give to people and that can really help them?"

The answer was obvious to both of us—Romantic relationships!

It was where my biggest personal transformation had occurred. It was where all my smart, PHD and master's degree educated girlfriends were still struggling. What if I decided to help these women with the messages that I had known to be true and charged for my time instead of doing it for free?

Then and there, the idea of 'Sami Wunder' was born!

It was like all the dots were connecting magically in that moment and I could not contain my excitement. I was going to be a love coach, specialising in helping high achieving women like myself find and keep true love.

4. Others May Not Understand And This Is Okay

The decision was made but it was not all hunky-dory from that point onwards.

For starters, nobody in my family understood who a love coach was and what the job role entailed. I consider myself a lucky woman because my partner, my in-laws and my own amazing parents and elder sister supported me with my decision.

For example, I remember my mom saying, *"I don't know what this is about but if this is the way you want to go, we trust you."*

Same with my father, he said, *"I would've ideally imagined you with a job at the European Central Bank but this is your life and I want to trust you with your decisions. You create magic wherever you go, because that is who you are."*

Christopher too has always been a champion for my dreams and desires.

And yet, I know this isn't the truth for so many women out there. You probably have an unsupportive family or spouse that makes you feel alone in your journey towards the pursuit of creating a true impact in the lives of others.

Worry not! It is not important that they get you, understand you or even agree with you. I had friends and family relatives who mocked me for quitting a lucrative career in economics to become a 'love coach.' For a lot of them, my choices were so radical and out-of-the-box that the only explanation they could find to understand my choices was that I had fared poorly in Economics and hence I was quitting it.

I remember wasting barely five minutes of my time and energy on wanting to prove to them that I was an excellent Economist, a gold medalist with well-paying offers for consultancy at a young age. And then I realised, what a waste of my time this would be because people believe what they want to believe. So, I decided to let all that 'noise' fade into the background and focused on what I wanted to create from an empowered space.

5. Use Your Empowered Energies to Turn Your Dreams Into Reality

Once the decision had been made, I had 10K savings in my bank account out of which I invested 8K to learn the skills of becoming a good coach.

Was that an easy decision? Not at all. I could've felt like a victim for giving away more than half of what I had saved in my bank account at 28 years of age and yet I decided to stay empowered around my decision. I took ownership of and stood by my dreams to make a big positive impact in the world. I decided to feel like the boss babe, the designer and creator of my own reality instead of feeling like a victim.

Over the months that followed, I opened a private Facebook group called 'Wunder Divas' that still exists today and started helping women with their love lives for free. I even charged 25 euros per session with my first ten clients in order to test and ensure that my process and tools were working. These women felt so lucky to have my time and in return I got testimonials from them, which then attracted more clients and referrals. The wheels started to spin quickly for me.

To me, what was most important in this journey of entrepreneurial success was that I was leading with results for my clients and creating a true positive impact in their lives, as I had promised to deliver. That is where my entire focus was at the start.

All of my first ten clients are today happily married, some of them even mothers to what we call 'Wunder babies.' I know my process works, as Í have now led over 300 women down the aisle and hundreds of others have attracted happily, committed relationships after going through my online programs.

The business grew into six figures in the first year itself, multi-six figures in the second year, 7 figures in the third year and I am so proud to share that today we run a multi-million-dollar company that serves women from across 55 countries of the globe to have happy, healthy romantic relationships. I've had to drastically increase my prices for my private time due to the high demand and requests I receive from clients.

And yet, I've been able to serve thousands across the globe through my easily downloadable online programs that are available at a fraction of the cost of my private time and have helped me serve one too many. We have helped women bring back marriages from the brink of divorce and reignited the spark and passion in hundreds of other relationships.

The next step to increasing my impact is releasing my first book in the market. It is called SOFT—and it lays out a new paradigm for romantic success for high achieving women.

I'd like to finish with the final message that adversity is where your real strength, commitment and resilience is tested. When the going gets tough, trust that it is opening the doors for something big in your life. Stay connected with that voice inside you that knows it is meant for something bigger. And before you know it, you will be walking right through that door to create the life of your dreams and service to others.

ABOUT THE AUTHOR

SAMI WUNDER

Sami Wunder is an internationally-recognized dating and relationship expert who specializes in working with high-achieving women professionals and entrepreneurs to attract their dream man and create a deeply intimate and deeply connected relationship.

Since 2016, over 300 of Sami's clients have found their happily-ever-after using Sami's method of soulmate attraction, and countless marriages and relationships have been saved and reconnected.

Such stellar results are unheard of in the industry. Sami's clients include a Hollywood celebrity, UK TV stars, CEOs, leading entrepreneurs and influencers and everyday women who care about the health of their relationships.

She's been hailed as the 'Get The Ring Coach' by the BBC Radio London and the Daily Mail, and her work has been picked up by the Time Magazine, Forbes Magazine and many other publications of global renown.

Sami is based in Europe and runs her heart-centered multi 7-figure company. She is blissfully married to the love of her life. They have two sons.

Find Sami on: www.samiwunder.com
Instagram: @samiwundercoach

Grab your free gift from Sami on: https://samiwundercoaching.lpages.co/lean-back-masterclass/

Website: http://samiwunder.com/

2

MARIA FONTANA

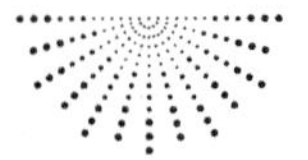

THE COURAGE TO REINVENT YOURSELF

After 14 years of amazingly wild success as an entrepreneur, I came to a screeching halt. It was like I had been hit by a train that I had been trying to hold back and could not move out of the way.

I found myself struggling with depression, overwhelmed, going through a toxic divorce with two young children and financially ruined from the aftermath of the split.

Now, don't get me wrong this is not a damsel in distress story, but rather a queen who was knocked off her throne from behind.

The level of stress and anxiety I was experiencing daily was unbearable, I was constantly at the doctor's office and even ER thinking I was having a heart attack, I could not sleep and could not stop eating, and felt the world crashing down upon me.

Just dealing with the process of divorce, losing my home and being left with tremendous debt was absolutely horrifying to me, "How did I allow this to happen to me, I had my shit together", I thought.

I struggled to keep a smile on my face and not let anyone know what was happening in my life, I was so ashamed and embarrassed, I felt so alone and vulnerable.

How could this be my life? I had it all, a six-figure business at 19,

I was a successful business owner, I was together, I was smart, I was ahead of the game, the ideal wife, business woman, daughter, the perfect everything to everybody but myself.

These questions tormented my soul and dragged me into a dark place of blame and shame, especially of what others may think, I began to feel anxious, overwhelmed and simply not good enough.

But little did I know this was what "hitting a wall" meant for me, and I was having a wakeup call to take action or die, a true Awakening as a matter of fact, an awakening of the shit hitting the fan for spiritual growth and energetic shifts that were so necessary in my life, even though I was still clueless why the hell this was happening.

After hitting rock-bottom, I knew I had to rebuild myself, life and business not only for me but for my children. My beautiful kids looked up to me, I had to get my act together at all costs, regardless of who's fault it was or the toxic karmic family coding would spill into another generation.

The thoughts and questions were met with massive overwhelm, fear of more loss and confusion, and what and how do I do this without any money or help? Would I be able to really do it?

This is where I looked within and asked the Universe and God for help. I did not know exactly where to start but I knew I had the power within and years of successful business experience and a strong energy to fall back on to fix my life and finances.

At that point I had been working on my own healing and personal development for a few years. It was rough for me, I had to address old baggage and family patterns that were holding me back, suffocating me. But this healing was pivotal in me finding the courage to go on and figure it all out.

One day at a time I took action toward reinventing myself and recovering my power!

I had lost all faith in myself for a short time. I was allowing outside forces to dictate my story, but I realized I was still a powerful being and had to dig out the courage to change my outcomes, so I started on my mission of rebuilding my business, life and finances.

This is where the power is, in ourselves, in our souls.

Looking back, I can clearly remember my grand opening of my first business. I was only 19 years old and no one had believed in me. I saved money working 3 jobs and launched my first business even though I really had no idea what I was doing. I only knew one thing for sure, I wanted to be the boss and have control over how I showed up in the world. It was so empowering, and I felt unstoppable, the feelings and strong visions unveiled a gift of manifesting what I desired, even though I had no idea what was happening.

So, I committed to being successful and I co-created a six figure salon in the early 90's, which was a huge accomplishment for a young woman in my early 20's. Then followed by 6 other successful brick and mortar businesses.

Fast forward 14 years and BAM, everything has changed. Well, if I say it happened overnight, I would be lying, it did seem to go in slow motion now that I think about it, isn't that the way it always seems?

So, I was taking care of a client one afternoon while in a dark place of despair, truly feeling like shit, disconnected and just not present in my body, when the divine stepped in to show me the way.

My client handed me a business card and said, "When you are ready, call her."

"Call who?" I thought.

This is when I began to hear the whispers from my soul, the clear messages from my intuition and started to take action toward recovery and healing, I had to take intentional action or else.

The miracle went a little like this. I became totally bored expecting the worst and ready to try something new that scared me. I called that number and began working with a healer aka (my therapist Norma) 2x a week.

Tiptoeing into the world of personal development and healing was not easy for me, I had no idea you could feel better or how much baggage I had been carrying and how heavy it was.

You see, I was raised by loving people but with limiting mindsets and beliefs that you never share your business, feelings or troubles with people, especially a therapist! Of course, I quickly learned I had to let that go and forgive everyone including myself. I had to shift my expectations and accept that blaming did nothing but hurt me and it was truly no fault of their own, they were simply doing the best they could with what they had at the moment, which is very true for so many people, we just do not know it.

Through my healing journey, I learned how powerful I truly was, and that I had an innate gift of intuition and insightful magic for figuring things out and creating clarity for others. This empowered me and gave me hope again.

I slowly and methodically started creating new rituals for myself including putting myself in my calendar for self-care, meditating, practicing morning gratitude and rewarding myself for every small goal I met, I was no longer available for negative people or anything that did not feel good. I also do not allow negative self-talk, or others to affect my outcomes. By learning how to create healthy boundaries, (this was not easy) which took me time to apply as a routine to my life, but honestly was a game-changer once it became second nature. Boundaries were pivotal in me becoming empowered again. Remember it takes 21 days to change a habit, so give the practice time.

Creating attainable goals was also key, you see when we overwhelm ourselves with enormous sized goals, we can fall off the wagon easier, I found creating bite size goals helped me dissect what and how to approach my weekly to do list. I began with getting clarity on what type of business I was going to start, it seemed obvious I would re-launch a salon because that was my primary practice for years, but I also had a burning desire for more, I had a vision of helping women globally start and grow their own businesses, I wanted to share that you can heal, manifest and live a life of abundance no matter what or where you come from, a marriage of personal and professional growth fuelled my mission. I desired all this goodness before I created my new business, so I got to work creating a game plan, a rough draft of sorts filled with clear visions, strategies and mindset shifts.

Over the years, people were always asking me if they could just "pick my brain" about how I did this or that, how I opened so many businesses, how I got financing, how I healed, how I was so empowered, how I got remarried to the love of my life, published 3 books, started a podcast, became a consultant, grew my businesses etc.

So, this is where I uncovered my magic. It was in sharing all my business experiences and growth strategies, both personal and professional, with a splash of my intuitive gifts and spirituality with the world that I was going to follow my new dream of creating impact, helping women start, launch and grow purpose driven businesses that offered them flexibility and financial freedom as an Intuitive business consultant.

One small step at a time I reverse engineered what I would need to launch my new practice and still pay my bills and support my kids at the same time.

So, I started by opening a studio/salon which was easy as pie for me because I had owned other larger businesses before, this would create the cash infusion to take care of my family and slowly reinvest in my new business.

In my 35-year entrepreneurial journey I have owned salons, tanning salons, a beauty distributorship, private label beauty brands and even a cab company and real estate investments, to say I am super diversified in business is an understatement.

Through strategic steps and careful planning, I was back in business for a few weeks, behind the chair, which was physically taxing on my body and mentally exhausting at times, but I did what I had to do and accelerated financially to pay down outrageous debt and start investing in mentors and a life coach including my healer to support my growth even more.

During times of adversity and challenge I have learned one thing for sure, we need to support, find a mentor, healer, clergy, therapist, coach or consultant, just invest in getting the support in whatever you need to grow, heal or accelerate, this is where the power is, it is never a sign of weakness but a sign of self-love and strength.

Going at it alone is lonely and hard, we cannot see the "label" from inside the bottle I learned, just find support at any cost. If you are on a tight budget, be creative, barter, exchange services or find someone who is aligned with your needs, everything is temporary, just remember that.

But this was simply a steppingstone in my bigger picture game-plan,

You see, I needed to have an income to live and take care of my kids while putting together my new consulting/coaching practice. This is a mistake I see many newer entrepreneurs make by not having an income or steady cash flow to invest in their business, building a business usually takes time and money in the real world, no exceptions. As I worked in my brick-and-mortar business I began to invest in further training and education of tactics and tech I was not an expert at, I took classes and courses, hired mentors and educated myself further, this intentional action created an energetic flow of things appearing and aligning perfectly for my vision to come together. Let me be crystal clear here, it was a lot of dedication and hard work, any business that is sustainable is work, but totally possible. You must believe everything is possible and ask yourself, "how can I do it"?

As I put my new practice together, I made many mistakes, which is totally normal and expected when you do something new. But, through patience and constantly working on and being honest with myself, I began to see my goals being reached. I can remember the excitement when I signed on to my first consulting client, I was absolutely thrilled. And even more ecstatic when she got more than the results she truly hired me for, and then many more success stories followed.

I was beyond grateful and have started to grow my business to be of the highest service to my beautiful clients and offer a life-changing transformation experience at all levels.

The most powerful part of this journey was always stepping out of my comfort zone, learning and doing new things that scared me. I did one thing a day that scared the crap out of me every single day (most of the time) and then rewarded myself for it. To be truly transparent here, I did fall off the wagon once in a while, but I just kept going, and I learned to be really nice to myself during the journey, no more negative shit talk to myself, I spoke to myself with the love I gave to everyone else for the first time in my life.

I was so happy to be on a mission that was not only helping me but would impact hundreds of women around the world one day, my intentions and vision were crystal clear, this is how ***Maria Fontana Consulting*** and the Business Growth Made Easy™ Methodology was born.

If I kept playing by the rules of people pleasing and putting myself second, I never would of gotten the support I needed to heal and grow, I never would of risked it all to save myself and reinvent my business, I never would of had such a powerful, transformational impact on so many amazing, big-hearted women globally.

In fact it was a blessing that I hit the wall, it was a blessing I had met my ex-husband and experienced such drama, it was a blessing to have my two children...who are true lights in my life and are catalyst for my continuing growth, it was an eye opening lesson to teach me what matters in this life and that we hold the power to create anything we truly desire with zero barriers.

We are limitless beings full of magic that can manifest absolutely all our dreams, no matter where we come from.

Today I find myself writing this chapter and my heart is so full, I am honoured to share a fragment of my story to motivate, inspire and empower you from the bottom of my heart. I am blessed with a successful consulting/coaching business that is elevating me and transforming thousands of women's lives and businesses globally, but the biggest win for me is that I can speak and share hope and direction from a place of love and true experience to help other women bring their desires and goals to fruition.

Remember, being compassionate, but unapologetic, what others say about you is none of your business, only apologizing if you are truly wrong, otherwise don't, surrender to the Spirit and have faith in something bigger than you.

Your epic life is waiting, be focussed on living your life purpose, that is how you are going to have the most positive impact versus fixating on negative crap.

Stay focused on the outcomes you desire and find mentors who are aligned and can support your mission from a deeper location of service. Remember to be kind to yourself, we are all humans and have a birth right to live in joy and abundance.

Wherever you may be in your journey, and regardless of where you are coming from, take a deep breath and remember why you started, remember the feelings of laughter, happiness and being fulfilled in your soul and then plan to expect miracles.

You are a powerful being with limitless capabilities and anything you truly hold an intention and desire for can be yours, release the limiting mindsets, create a plan, find support and make your dreams your reality, you got this!

Love & Light Maria Fontana

ABOUT THE AUTHOR

MARIA FONTANA

Maria Fontana is a leading Women's Empowerment & Business Consultant who works with Extraordinary Female Entrepreneurs helping them create their own success as a feminine leader.

She helps them get utter clarity and create a game plan so that they can kick start their service based or expert consultancy business with Aligned Energy, Positive Mindsets and Proven Business Strategies.

She has spent 3 decades as an entrepreneur and mentor coaching, teaching, inspiring and motivating thousands of people around the world.

Her practical, no-nonsense advice and proven business strategies provide tangible results and major positive shifts for her global clients. Her Intuitive emotional intelligence has a powerful impact bringing forth clarity and abundance.

She lives in New Jersey with her two children and husband.

She loves Italy, fine wine and cooking.

Website: https://mariafontana.com/

3

MELANIE MACINTYRE

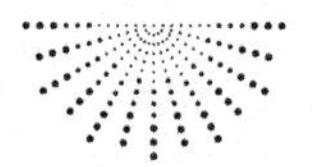

BECOMING WILDLY AWAKENED: THE POWER OF POST TRAUMATIC GROWTH AND HOW TO HARNESS IT FOR YOUR FUTURE

I woke up to my alarm ringing like a warning bell of impending doom and immediately felt the all too familiar pit of despair that seemed to have taken up squatters rights in my stomach. I could instantly feel the tears start to prickle my eyes like pins and needles and then inevitably they started to slide down my face creating a pool of resigned misery on my pillow. I felt utterly soaked in fear and trapped in a groundhog day-like existence as I tried to pull myself together to face the day.

Today was not a day I could lie there and feel sorry for myself however, I was on a schedule that couldn't be moved. I took a deep breath, swung my legs out of bed and got up to face the day. I walked about 5 steps and caught a glimpse of myself in the mirror and stopped in my tracks. I crumpled to the floor in a broken heap and felt the most curious sensation of emptiness. There was nothing left. There was nothing left to draw on to get through today. There wasn't a single ounce of energy left for me to cling onto to fuel my positive self-talk to get me through what I had to face. The very last flicker of the flame of hope, positivity and life force energy that lived in my solar plexus had gone out.

I looked at myself in the mirror and didn't know who was staring back at me. She had my hair, and resembled someone I was supposed to know intimately, but her spark was gone. Her eyes were cloudy and filled with the shadows of fear, resignation and exhaustion. She looked haunted and lost, like a little girl I once knew.

My mind immediately dragged me back to the present moment - '*What are you going to do?*' screamed my inner voice. "*How will you get through today? You can't let anyone down, there are too many people depending on you. Your dad needs you to step up and be his strength today. You need to step up to the plate and stick to your project plan. You are in the middle of making your team redundant. You need to deal with it.*'

I took a moment to steady myself and something inside me said '*Stop*'. But it was a different voice to the one that was screaming, it sounded like a whisper but something about it sounded and felt more authoritative than the other voice. There was a quiet power behind it that I couldn't ignore. I leaned into it and kept listening.

'*Stop. You don't 'need' to do* ***anything*** *other than show up for yourself and your dad today. The rest can wait.*'

I felt a strange sensation of calm and relief flood through me as I attached to the possibility of this course of action. Then, before my intensely critical inner voice could talk me out of it, I made a decision. I would take my dad to hospital today to get half of his cancerous lungs removed and then instead of going into work to continue the process of making my team redundant and restructuring the function I led I would come back home and wait until my dad was out of his operation. I'd then go back to the hospital to be with him. I would allow myself some space and grace to deal with how scared I felt about his cancer being back for a second time and also give him the gift of my full presence when he needed me most.

The date was 30th May 2014. It was the day the trajectory of my life changed inconceivably. It was the day I began to listen to my soul and let her lead the way.

From this moment on, life as I knew it quickly began to unravel.

One day off work gave me just enough time to realise that I needed another. I went to see my doctor, hoping for some sympathy and compassion. What I got was logic, a strict talking to and a very direct challenge - 'I could sign you off for 2 weeks but there is something much more fundamental going on here. You need to have a discussion with your boss.'

My mind immediately flashed to my wonderful boss and the pit of angry snakes in my stomach leapt and writhed like someone was holding a flame too close to them. The fear at the thought of 'letting her down' was almost unbearable. I loved my leader. She saw potential in me and supported me to be promoted into my senior leadership role. How could I fail her? My heart raced and I felt like I would vomit.

'Now, I want to put you back on medication and antidepressants starting today.'

Oh, I was still at the doctors. I was prepared for this and I had my answer ready. 'I think I can do this on my own. I think I know what I need to do to heal from this and get better. I want to try to heal my depression and anxiety and stomach problems by making changes and taking better care of myself.'

My doctor was not enamoured with this suggestion and continued to tell me all the reasons why I should go back on antidepressants. But I was adamant. 'Give me time', I said 'and let me try. If it doesn't work I'll come back for the pills.'

And so began my long road home to myself. My healing journey, which was to give me more than I ever could have imagined and through which I would lose more than I could bear to contemplate.

My mind was tired and broken from a lifetime of self-flagellation, intense inner criticism and constant trying - trying to be all things to all people except for myself. The people pleasing perfectionist in me was strong and she was not going to let go of me without a fight.

Organisational culture and constraints and a very masculine dominated environment within my corporate career kept me faking it to fit in. I lacked a deep, inner confidence in myself and my abilities. I would sit at the board room table feeling like a 'silly little girl' afraid to speak up, always wondering when I would get found out. My Imposter Syndrome was constantly fed and watered by the daily environment I worked in.

My overreliance on my logical mind and left brain meant I was constantly questioning myself and getting stuck in analysis paralysis. My inner critic was a mean bitch who fed me the same old stories of why I was a failure. This constant diet of criticism and self-doubt was crippling my ability to perform and lead and destroying my confidence.

Amongst it all was this gnawing sensation that lived in my belly that when I felt into it was a deep, deep yearning. A yearning to make a meaningful difference. To fulfill some bigger purpose, even though at that point I had zero idea what my purpose was!

As I walked away from my life as I knew it to start over. I only knew 2 things:

- I needed to do work that made a meaningful difference in the world and helped people
- I had no idea how that would look or how I would make it happen but I knew I would work it out

Little did I know the most magical chapter of my life was about to begin in all of my abject misery. My soul had decided 'enough was enough' and was about to get serious with me and not give up until I began to listen.

And so in my torment and confusion about my life and how miserable I was in the way I was living it began the start of my spiritual awakening.

An awakening to who I truly am and what I am here to do.

An awakening of what I love and who I am here to serve.

An awakening to my truest talents and most impactful qualities that I am here to share with the world to make it a brighter, better, more loving place.

The awakening of the parts of me that I had ignored, silenced and stuffed down and the start of my journey back home to myself as I tentatively began to get to know my soul.

And ultimately, to the awakening of five profound lessons that have become the lifeblood of my business...

Lesson One: Your soul is always nudging you, guiding you and showing you the way. When you don't listen, life will unfold (often through challenges) to make sure you do.

Within a few months I had completely dismantled my life as I knew it to take a break. I left my job, moved out of our beautiful flat, put all of our furniture in storage and booked 2 tickets to travel around Asia for six months with my partner Charlie.

My dad had recovered well from his operation and didn't need any additional treatment and each day, as we focused on his health and recuperation, he grew stronger.

We had recently bought a house on the little island where he grew up in Eriskay in the Outer Hebrides of Scotland. It was always his dream to retire there and now he had a home of his own again. He had been living with me for a few years during his cancer treatments which was a lot of fun but he needed his own place to call home.

I wasn't out of the woods with my physical and mental health but I was feeling a strong sense of possibility about our future and I knew our travelling adventure was just what I needed to kickstart my own next chapter.

Charlie and I set off for Nepal where we were starting our trip by trekking in the Himalayas and attending a yoga retreat. I spent the next 6 months healing my mind, body and soul. We were both reading and learning voraciously. Me about psychology, neuroscience, quantum physics and the link between science and spirituality.

Charlie in physiology, nutrition and physical health. We would talk long into the day and night about what we had learned that day and help each other to connect the dots between mind, body and soul and living a life at your maximum capacity and potential.

I committed to new habits I had always flirted with. Meditation, journaling, yoga, regular exercise and movement, time in nature appreciating the beauty of the world. As I leaned more into this way of being present and connected each day, an ancient memory awoke within me: we were part of nature and not separate from it - people and planet all interconnected. With this new flow of wisdom and clarity along with my new habits and routines that supported me to thrive, I began to heal at a very fundamental level and we came back focused and ready to build a new life for ourselves. I had found a way to live my life from my head AND my heart and learned to loosen the lifelong, crippling grip of anxiety and depression by resetting my nervous system and opening up the lines of communication with my heart and soul.

Lesson Two: ***'Being' is just as important as 'doing' in creating success and fulfilling your potential.***

Learning to 'be you' through habits and practices that strengthen the connection to your inner wisdom and not feel the need to constantly be 'doing' is such a profound and simple shift. With the right habits and routines, you can release the grip of your overactive mind and the guilt and self criticism that comes with it. This is the secret to healing your body and tapping into all the resources available to you to become a healthier, happier, more awakened version of yourself with ease. It's also what keeps you out of overwhelm and in the space of inspiration as you create the life and future you deeply desire.

By the time we came home I had clarity that I wanted to start up my own business as a coach. I had been coaching my team, clients and executives throughout my professional career for 16 years and had always been passionate about helping people unlock their deeper potential and create more success. Now I wanted to do that on my terms without being part of a corporate or organisational machine. I decided to invest in myself through a new coaching certification and came across an opportunity that looked very exciting and more than a little scary - travelling to California to be trained by the best performance coach in the world, learning a science backed methodology to help people radically increase their ability to succeed with ease. It was perfect! I was accepted as a new coach to the programme and came back from the USA brimming with excitement and a business plan to sign up my first clients within the following weeks.

Everything was working out perfectly. I invested in working with a business mentor I really admired by joining a mastermind programme in the USA and signed up my first client as if by magic. I was flying high as everything began to unfold beyond my wildest dreams.

But life sometimes has its own ideas and two weeks after I signed up my first coaching client I was served a curveball that destroyed my world in a moment.

'Mr MacIntyre, the cancer has returned and is on your spine and your femur and is inoperable. I'm afraid we cannot offer any treatment to cure at this stage, only delay the spread.'

And in an instant my world fell apart as my dad received his final, terminal cancer diagnosis.

Everything I had learned was tested to the max.

When my dad was diagnosed for the third and final time with cancer, we chose to fight. We wouldn't accept that it was his time to die (as he made the mistake of telling me he wasn't ready!) The truth is, I wasn't ready either. We cashed in on a life assurance policy and took off to Germany for him to receive treatment. We were filled with hope which is a powerful currency when trying to stay alive. More tests followed to understand the effectiveness of the new treatment. The moment I had to tell my dad he was going to die is one I will never forget. He turned away from me, trying to shut himself and his pain away from me. The whole time he was sick I tried to protect him too by doing the same.

I was struck in that moment by the absolute necessity for us both to let our guards down, and drop the protective shields we had spent lifetimes perfecting and polishing to protect each other from witnessing the other's hurt. We had to open up to each other and share the immensity of our pain. And we had to do it together.

But the fear was real - to open up to him and face this together was to open up the floodgates to a tsunami of pain and suffering that most of us spend our whole lives trying to avoid.

It seems counterintuitive but I knew feeling more pain through doing this together and witnessing the full extent of each other's worst kind of heartache would ultimately lead to more healing.

And it did.

For the next 5 months (he still lived a lot longer than expected!) we showed up for each other in ways we never had and we lived full out.

I learned to ask for help when all I wanted to do was carry him and care for him alone.

I learned a humility that can only come from seeing someone suffer with such courage and fortitude.

I experienced grace that is born from caring for another human with more tenderness and gentleness than I knew was possible.

We developed a gratitude for life, each other and the glory of love that would not otherwise have been possible if we had not made that decision to turn face on to each other's suffering in our darkest moments.

My dad's suffering and his death were the greatest gifts he bestowed upon me.

Because witnessing his suffering and learning to be the woman, daughter and carer that was by his side to be present and ease his passing is my greatest achievement in life.

I found a level of peace and acceptance in myself through his death that I never knew were possible.

I learned how to transmute pain and suffering and turn it into strength and grace and gratitude.

It was hard to put my baby business to one side but in a moment of clarity I realised my greatest calling was to step up and serve my dad to the best of my ability. When I came out the other side I would be forever changed and deeply healed and prepared for any challenges I encountered building my business.

Lesson Three: ***In your darkest moments lie your greatest opportunities for growth and transformation if you can lean into them and be supported to learn the wisdom available to you.***

When my dad was nearing the end, I talked to him about my dreams for the work I was learning I was here to do. How the journey we had been on together and the strength of his love would live through the transformation I would help others to achieve.

As with my own story and experience, my clients have often gone through difficulties or challenges in their own lives which have led them to feel a deep sense of purpose and determination to make a difference. (The psychological term for this phenomenon is Post Traumatic Growth).

My clients are the bravest and most inspirational people I know as they are determined to support and serve others through spreading the wisdom and insight they have gained through their own challenges and experiences. I often hear their dreams and desires to help others just like them to move forward and create the transformation and change they know are possible through overcoming their own challenging chapters. They are willing to take a leap into the unknown, start a new chapter and create a business that will help them shine their light brightly in the world by helping others.

Lesson 4: ***You can use your challenges to your advantage and create a new chapter.***

A business is the perfect vehicle to realise your purpose and use your unique insights, wisdom, experience and talents to create the change you wish to see in the world. In my work I help clients awaken to their mission and fully claim it. I help them know exactly what their game plan needs to be to get there. And I help them learn new habits, routines, business strategies and tools that will support them to transform and become the leader their mission and purpose requires them to be. It never ceases to amaze me what we are capable of as human beings when we tap into the wisdom that resides within us and use the challenges we face to our advantage and the advantage of others.

So the final lesson I want to leave you with:

Lesson Five: ***You are not meant to do this on your own.***

There is a transformational force within the power of community and allowing yourself to be supported, and in my experience coaching is the most powerful tool you can use to unlock the answers you need to become everything you are destined to be.

One thing I know for sure is your life has and will provide you with every lesson you need to fulfill your potential, self-actualise and serve at your highest level: To Become Wildly Awakened. I hope when you are faced with your own darkest moments you can draw on the lessons from this chapter. I know it will help you open up the gateway to your own greatness and may be the path to your own Wildly Awakened Business.

ABOUT THE AUTHOR

MELANIE MACINTYRE

Mel MacIntyre is an Intuitive Business Coach who works with women who are awakening to their true purpose and are being called to make a difference through their business.

She helps them to connect with their unique mission and lead from their heart using a blend of intuitive, psychological and business strategies so that they can get out of overwhelm, release their fears of being judged and becoming visible, fully realise their potential and create a world changing impact.

Mel has been personally trained by and worked for the world's best performance coach and is a trained intuitive coach. She is an Ambassador for Women's Enterprise in Scotland using her voice to represent and promote women and their interests in business and has been featured in the Guardian and BBC along with many more publications.

Mel lives in the Outer Hebrides of Scotland with her partner Charlie and son Maximilian.

Website: www.melmacintyre.com

4

DINA BEHRMAN

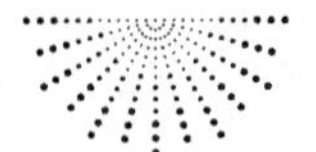

FINDING MY VOICE

I stared at the computer screen and blinked in disbelief. 'Yes, I'd love to interview you,' read the email. 'This would be perfect for my Forbes column.'

What the heck? I was going to be interviewed and featured in Forbes! Yes, this self-confessed introvert and regular sufferer of Imposter Syndrome was going to be written about in a major publication.

I felt an overwhelming sense of pride and happiness. This was it, I'd finally put myself out there. I'd finally stopped being scared to just go for it. I'd finally decided enough was enough, I was done playing small.

Born in January, I was a typical Capricorn – down-to-earth, a little bit serious, diligent, and sometimes introspective.

My parents like to tell the story of how I was so quiet at kindergarten that the teachers used to have to pretend to wind me up like a clockwork toy to get me to speak.

As I grew older I became less quiet, but was still a heads-down-and-get-on-with-it kind of school pupil and never one of the loud, outspoken ones.

But whilst I may not have been one to speak up, I soon discovered I could express myself another way – through writing.

I started writing stories, scribbling them down in pencil-lined exercise books. I wrote letters, lists, recipes - I just loved writing.

And I started reading anything I could get my hands on. Reading and writing became my escape. I would write about magical worlds and places I'd never been, I'd let my imagination run away with me.

In secondary school, when the teachers arranged work experience placements for us I desperately wanted to do mine at the local newspaper, but instead I was sent to do an admin job at a nearby office. So when the school holidays arrived I contacted the newspaper myself and arranged my own work experience with them.

I spent the week shadowing their journalists, watching them conduct interviews and write up stories. The idea that I could be paid to write articles and tell people's stories for a living seemed wild. Here was an opportunity to be creative and express myself, and get paid.

That week of work experience cemented my desire to become a journalist. I knew that it was my destiny to write for a living and share people's stories.

I tore open the envelope and scanned the letter from my local newspaper. "We're sorry to tell you that your application for the reporter role has not been successful." It felt like a punch in the gut. It wasn't the first time I'd been turned down for a journalism job. It was such a competitive industry that even getting work experience was a challenge, with many publications booked up for a year or more in advance.

But I knew I couldn't let it put me off. A couple of months later I sent another letter to the same local paper, asking if any other roles had come up. This time I got a positive response! They wanted me to come and do maternity cover for their editorial assistant. It was an admin role, but as they knew I was keen to write, they said they'd let me do some writing too. Not only that, if it all went well they'd pay for me to do my journalism training. I was ecstatic, I knew this was the start of something big.

At the paper I got involved with as much writing as possible. I introduced myself to a local magazine editor in the same office and started writing for her too. I did my training and became a qualified reporter. Then I went on to do my senior reporter exams. I learnt so much working at the paper. I went to court and reported on different cases, I interviewed celebrities who were visiting the area – I even interviewed the Prime Minister at one point. I spoke to people from all walks of life and helped them to tell their stories.

After a couple of years I started getting itchy feet. I loved magazines, reading the likes of Marie Claire and Cosmopolitan had always been an indulgence of mine, and I had dreamt of writing for a magazine. When my friend Katie started doing shifts on a showbiz magazine she told me they needed more writers. So I started using my days off from the paper to work in-house doing shifts for the magazine. Gradually I built up my experience until I was ready to leave the paper.

But whilst work was going well, behind the scenes I was struggling with some difficult family stuff.

It was the day after my 25th birthday that my Dad took an overdose. The ambulance rushed him to hospital and the nurse ushered my mum and I into a special side room for family. "Wait here, the Doctor will be out to speak to you soon," she said. Minutes passed, or was it hours? It felt like forever.

We spent the next week sitting by his bedside, watching the lines on the monitors going up and down.

Gradually my Dad started recovering physically. Mentally however, things started getting worse. Eventually he was admitted to a psychiatric hospital. He was severely depressed, and started having psychotic episodes, where he experienced paranoia and delusions.

It was such a stressful and worrying time, but it was difficult to tell people what was going on. I couldn't just call them up and tell them what was happening, it felt too awkward and uncomfortable to talk about.

I remember feeling so alone at that time and I remember thinking *I wish I could hear from someone who's been through this, I just want to know that this is something I can get through and come out the other side of.*

One day, when the time is right, I'll write about this, I told myself, so that I can help anyone else going through something similar.

After a few years working on different showbiz magazines, I landed a job as Commissioning Editor at a national newspaper supplement. I was working three days a week in the office, with two days a week to myself to focus on freelancing.

I was in charge of the 'Real Life' section of the magazine and commissioned stories about people from all walks of life.

My inbox was constantly inundated with emails from people wanting to be featured but we only had spots for two features a week, so I quickly became very good at spotting a good headline and a newsworthy story angle.

On my days off, I started focusing on writing health features for national newspapers. I loved being able to really dive into learning about a subject, researching it and interviewing case studies and experts.

But after two years in my job, following a round of redundancies, I was told they no longer had any work for me. Initially, I felt devastated—but I soon realized where one door closes, another door opens. This was my chance to make a full time living as a freelance journalist. It was quite a scary proposition, but it was exciting.

At first, I had to get used to being on the other side of the fence; I was the one pitching the editors with the overflowing inboxes and initially this proved to be quite hard. I'd either get 'thanks, but no thanks' responses or my emails would go completely ignored. I realized I needed to perfect my pitching skills. It took trial and error, but eventually I nailed it and became published in virtually every national UK newspaper and several magazines.

I loved helping people to share their stories, to get their voices heard. After a while I realised it was time for me to share my own story. By this point my Dad was a lot better so, with his blessing, I pitched a piece to a glossy women's magazine about having a parent with mental health issues. I wrote about his breakdown, the overdose, the depression, psychosis, all of it, and the impact it had had on me as his daughter. Writing it was truly cathartic, although it felt uncomfortable sharing something so personal and being so vulnerable. I'd always been such a private person, so opening up like this was massively out of my comfort zone.

But I remembered my younger self, and how much I had longed to hear from someone else who had been through something similar. If this helps just one person it will be worth it, I told myself.

The following month the magazine published a letter to the editor from a reader thanking them for running my article – she said she'd been going through something similar and reading my article had massively helped her. In that moment I knew it had all been worth it.

I continued with the journalism work, but soon I decided I needed to diversify. I took a course in copywriting and set myself up as a sole trader, offering PR and copywriting services. After ten years of journalism, I decided to wind down that side of things and focus on running my own business.

Initially I made every rookie mistake in the book: I didn't know who my ideal clients were, I didn't have strong boundaries in place, I took on anyone and everyone who wanted to work with me, and I massively undercharged, meaning I ended up overworked and underpaid. It was a big learning curve.

A few years passed. When my eldest daughter was born, I took some time out, and when I came back to work I had a renewed sense of purpose. I realized my real passion lay in teaching business owners how to do their own PR. I was ready to stop playing small and get myself out there. I hired a business coach, rebranded and re-launched as a PR coach.

My clients started achieving amazing results. But I still wasn't putting myself out there the way I could have been. If anything, I was hiding. I was suffering from Imposter Syndrome, and often felt that at any given moment I was going to be found out as a fraud.

When my business coach asked me, "What resource do you have that you're not using?" it hit me: I needed to start practicing what I preach and get visible. It was time to find my voice.

I started getting out there and truly owning my expertise. And I started pitching myself and getting featured in well-known publications. I had successfully pitched a client to Forbes and the reaction she got when the piece came out was fantastic. *Hmm, maybe I should try pitching myself to Forbes?* I thought to myself. Before I would never have had the guts to do it. Previously I would have listened to those little voices in my head saying, *'Who are you to be featured in Forbes?'* or *'Why would anyone be interested in what you have to say?* and *'You're not successful enough/well known enough/you don't have a big enough following'.* But this time I ignored the mind monkeys.

I sent off a pitch and, when I heard back that the journalist wanted to feature me, it felt amazing! I'd always thought big media coverage was for other people, not me. But now I realised it was my turn.

Sharing that Forbes feature when it came out felt incredible. I had so many positive comments, messages of support, and connection requests because of it. I got offered a paid speaking gig, I had people contact me about wanting to work with me, I had people booking in 'discovery calls' with me.

I continued putting myself out there, writing for well-known publications as a PR expert and being interviewed on podcasts.

I started seeing results in my business as a direct result of being featured.

"I heard you being interviewed on a podcast and I just loved your energy," said one prospective client on a call. "I just knew I wanted to hire you."

Another time I opened my email: "Would love to work with you!" read the subject line. "I read your article and I heard your training and I'd love to sign up as a private client."

I landed thousands of dollars' worth of business by getting featured in the press and positioning myself as an expert.

The more I put myself out there, the more I reaped the rewards.

After my second daughter was born a few years later, my business continued to grow. Successful 7-figure entrepreneurs started hiring me as a publicist to do their PR for them. I had so much work, I had to hire freelance PRs to support me. I was super busy and my clients were being featured all over the place – Forbes, Business Insider, Marie Claire, BBC, Fox News.

Doing this work made my heart sing. I was helping these businesswomen share their inspiring stories and expertise in the press, enabling them to share their message with hundreds of thousands of people all over the world. And they were experiencing massive growth in their businesses as a result, often securing thousands of dollars-worth of business after being featured, as well as landing TED talks, magazine columns, radio shows and book deals. One client brought in ten new clients from just one article, another had a successful five-figure launch on the back of an article, another brought in 1500 leads and several high-ticket sales after being featured.

After a while, however, I decided it was time to close down my Done For You services and really pare down what I was offering in my business to focus on semi-passive income streams. I created a self-paced course, PR Power, to teach business owners at any stage of business how to do their own PR, and I created a PR Mastermind for those higher-level business owners to support them getting featured without having to do it all for them. Later, I launched my own publishing company, producing multi-author books for business owners. Fundamentally, my passion has always been to tell people's stories, or to empower them to tell them, and this remains the same to this day.

Often when I talk to people about sharing their story in a book or in the press they're worried about putting themselves out there. There are so many introverted entrepreneurs, and so many people who want to share their message more widely, but are scared about getting visible. Having been on my journey, I feel blessed that I get to guide these people on how they can get visible in a way that feels good to them.

In a world where we are constantly bombarded with noise, especially in the online space, this isn't about having to shout the loudest. This is about knowing that you have the power to genuinely help others by sharing your story, your expertise and your message. And understanding that by using powerful platforms like the media or a bestselling book to amplify your voice, the people who need to hear from you will do.

As Philip Pullman said: "After nourishment, shelter, and companionship, stories are the thing we need the most in the world."

ABOUT THE AUTHOR

DINA BEHRMAN

Former journalist-turned-PR strategist and publisher Dina Behrman works with entrepreneurs who want to stop being the internet's best kept secret and become the go to expert in their field. She empowers them to share their stories in bestselling books, and to leverage the media so they can create a much bigger impact in the world. She launched her business following a decade working as a journalist, during which she was published in virtually every national UK newspaper and many magazines. She's worked as a publicist for a number of 7-figure business owners, and has also helped hundreds of entrepreneurs learn how to do their own PR. She's been featured as a PR expert in Forbes, Entrepreneur, Huff Post, The Guardian, BBC radio, amongst others. She lives in the UK with her husband, two daughters and cat, Bobble.

Access PR & publishing resources:
https://dinabehrman.com/resources/
Website: www.dinabehrman.com

5

CASSIE MORRIS-DALTON

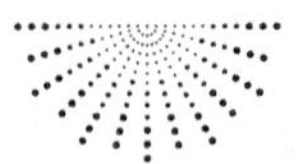

FROM BURNOUT TO BOSS: YOU CAN HAVE SUCCESS WITHOUT THE STRESS

Believe it or not, my life was saved by a French Bulldog. The best part? It wasn't even my dog!

If you can relate to what I'm going to talk about in this chapter, I'm so sorry. I know how heavy that weight on your shoulders is right now. Hopefully as you read this, you'll realise that you're not alone and maybe by the end, that load will feel a little lighter.

I wish I could remember the exact moment it happened. As I'm writing this, I feel as though I'm letting you down by not being able to recall what triggered it. In the grand scheme of things it doesn't really matter though, all that matters is that it happened.

One minute I was standing with my friend in the checkout line at Home Bargains, the next someone had turned the Earth's spin cycle up to eleven and cut off my oxygen supply. I was suffocating. My friend was saying something, babbling on as if nothing was wrong. Couldn't he see that I was on the verge of collapsing? My chest tightened. I couldn't tell if my heart was dancing the Cha Cha or about to come to an emergency stop.

The scene around me changed. The fluorescent overhead lights dimmed, casting elongated shadows over the gathering faceless crowd. The shelving doubled, tripled, in height yet paradoxically the ceiling was only inches from the floor.

Legs shaking, I staggered to the exit, leaving my friend to pay for my shopping. Maybe I said something to him, maybe I didn't. At that moment, I didn't care. All that mattered was finding an open space so I could catch my breath.

That's when I saw him—my handsome four-legged hero.

He confidently trotted over and sniffed at my shoes. I reached down and ruffled his fur, fingers trembling.

Then, for no logical reason, it stopped. I was fine.

The world stopped spinning. The oxygen was turned back on and my heart returned to normal. My legs were still jelly but hey, you can't have everything, right?

It was like waking up for the first time. Not just because stroking the bulldog had distracted me from the biggest anxiety attack of my life, it was as though I was seeing everything else from a new perspective.

Like I had just cleaned my glasses and suddenly the words weren't blurry anymore.

I could see all of the pieces of my life mapped out in front of me. They were a mess! Some areas of my life were crumbling, others were huge piles of rubble, some were completely on fire.

Things had to change. This, whatever this was, was not thriving. My pursuit for success was killing me.

Five minutes and £80 later my friend returned.

"Are you OK?" He asked.

"I need help," I said.

Up until that point I had felt fine. Not really, I just told everyone I felt fine because that's what everyone wants to hear, isn't it?

Let's get some perspective: I was working sixty (plus) hours a week as a teacher and on the side, I had launched a fitness coaching business (another twenty hours minimum). Having suffered with thyroid problems from the age of thirteen, I knew how much people struggled with their weight and self-esteem. It had been my dream to help other women going through the same thing and learn to love themselves while maintaining a healthy weight.

On top of that, I was determined to have a social life and keep myself fit (because who would hire an out of shape fitness coach?), perform with my ukulele as much as possible and be a responsible dog mum to my own Frenchie. It doesn't take a genius to realise that there were not enough hours in the day.

I was the poster girl for "hustle culture." In other words, I believed that the harder you worked, the more success you would have.

Every morning I would wake up (that's not quite true, I barely slept - I wore insomnia like a badge of honour, so I'll rephrase that) I would go from lying down with my eyes closed to standing with my eyes less closed, then rush out of the door, jump in the car and head to work. That was the only way I could function, if I gave myself time to think, anxiety would take over.

It was a poor coping mechanism.

On several occasions I remember thinking to myself that if the car were to skid off the road it would be better than facing the day ahead. Not that I wanted to hurt myself in any way. It was just that the idea of not having to face work for a few days, even a few hours, seemed better than the alternative.

Apparently, those kinds of intrusive thoughts are normal but if you are experiencing them, please talk to someone.

Things at work were dreadful. I spent my breaks either answering client messages or hiding in the classroom cupboard fighting back tears of frustration. There was no respite.

With hindsight it's no wonder I broke down.

It took me five weeks to recover from the incident in Home Bargains. Five full weeks of CBT, antidepressants and an incredible app called Wysa, which acts like a counsellor but without you having to open up to another human being, if you like me that's something you're worried about.

This downtime also gave me ample opportunity to evaluate what I really wanted to achieve out of life.

Turns out, hustling twenty-four-seven wasn't it!

Nor was teaching—I loved teaching, but the increasing pressure on teachers, especially now in post pandemic England, is ridiculous. I can't and won't speak for all teachers but in my opinion the education sector seems to care less and less about a child's education and welfare and more and more about check boxes and red tape. It wasn't the career I'd signed up for.

That left me with coaching, but there was a dark pattern emerging in that area too.

During my recovery I decided to document my journey on social media. I'd love to tell you I did that for selfless reasons, but honestly, it was for accountability and to prove to the nosy parkers at work that I was genuinely sick.

What I didn't anticipate was the sheer volume of other coaches, consultants and freelancers who came forward and expressed how they were suffering in the same way. It was truly heartbreaking.

Many shared how they had hit rock bottom. Even more said that they were on the verge of giving up on their dream of being their own boss because the pressure was too great.

To the outsider, the answer seems simple - give up the hustle, have a regular career with stability and predictability. Use the time you spent on your business relaxing with a hobby.

For us entrepreneurial types though, that's not how it really works. First of all, we get into business because working a "normal" job is incredibly challenging for us. Not in the sense that the work is difficult, but in the sense that we need more. We want the freedom and creativity being our own boss provides. We live and breathe for the challenge and growth. It's a different type of stress. Secondly, giving up on something you invested so much money and time in is not only one of the most difficult decisions to make emotionally and logically, it has a psychological impact too.

So many of these coaches I spoke to said that they felt worthless. They felt like they weren't capable enough. That even after working sixteen hours a day (or more) they felt like they still weren't working hard enough. Some started to believe that they just weren't good enough to follow their true passion and were terrified that if they couldn't do that, what else was there? Not only did they have to deal with the heartbreak of sacrificing something they had poured their heart and soul into creating, they also felt like they were failing themselves. Even more than that, they felt that they had let down the very people that had supported them as they struggled. To make matters worse, they also had to face the pompous gloating of the "I told you so" brigade.

Quitting runs so much deeper than pride. It becomes a part of who you are. You label yourself "a quitter", "a loser", or "not capable". You live constantly under the shadow of "what if?" It's not as easy as just going back to working a nine-to-five. It changes the very fabric of your identity and that affects every single aspect of your life. It means you are more likely to quit on your new exercise routine, more likely to give up on your healthy lifestyle, more likely to drop out of new hobbies (you know, the ones you now have time for). This happens because your brain loves consistency. In other words, if you identify as a failure, your brain is going to make damn sure that you live up to that label.

Here's the harsh truth about those who dream about being their own boss: we are our businesses—its success is our success. Equally, its failure is our failure. Separating the two is like separating salt from the ocean—entirely possible, but extremely difficult. Is that healthy? Probably not, but it's who we are.

Hearing all of the stories from those desperate coaches is what inspired me to pivot my mission. The idea of people having to choose between their dreams or their health was insane! It didn't sit right with me. Surely it didn't need to be an "and/or" situation. Did success really have to go hand in hand with stress? I had to do something. So I did some digging.

What separated those who flourished in business from those who floundered?

The answer soon became abundantly clear.

It wasn't the amount of hours you put in. It wasn't the skills you possessed. It wasn't the tools or the strategy or the knowledge.

None of those things meant Jack in the long run.

The key determiner of a successful business owner was their mindset. More specifically, their resilience and level of optimism.

The more I researched, the more I knew that I was on the right path. If I could teach these overwhelmed coaches how to optimise their mindset for success, they would have the tools within themselves to make their dreams a reality.

That's when I discovered Positive Psychology, the missing piece to my puzzle, and immediately enrolled in a course with the University of Pennsylvania.

Nicknamed the Science of Happiness, practicing positive psychology has been shown to increase a person's wellbeing, productivity, creativity and success. What's more, studies indicate that, by becoming "learned optimists," marketers actually increased their sales substantially compared to their pessimistic peers despite having the same amount of training. It turned out that happy people really do make more money.

So how can you become more optimistic?

First of all, let's ditch the belief that optimism is only for the naive. I see so many people claim they're realists, because in all honesty, it's just not cool to be optimistic. It's associated with immaturity, as if being an optimist makes you less rational or capable of free will. It's also tainted by the dangerously popular culture of toxic positivity being promoted on social media at the moment - that is the belief that we need to be positive all of the time or else we won't succeed!

The opposite is true. Picture this. When you feel down, what does your body tend to do? It closes itself off. It withdraws. You walk with your head down. Your thinking becomes very insular. Pessimism narrows your field of vision and the focus becomes more about yourself and less on the world around you, meaning you miss opportunities that are right in front of you. This isn't necessarily a bad thing. In fact it's how humans have evolved. We're naturally bad weather thinkers because in the early stages of our evolution we had to be in order to survive! However, we don't need to rely on that skill set anymore.

Optimism, on the other hand, challenges that old way of thinking. When you feel happy you walk with your head held high. You take in more of the world around you and this opens you up to more opportunities. Can you see how valuable that is when it comes to achieving success?

There is a positive psychology strategy I want to share with you today to equip you with the tools to become more optimistic so you can feel more fulfilled and ultimately increase your ability to thrive in whatever area you choose.

I want to show you how to identify pessimistic thinking patterns and replace them with optimistic ones. This is the exact exercise that helped me as I was recovering from my breakdown and is the same strategy I share with my clients to empower them too.

Imagine you're having one of *those* days. You know the ones where everything keeps going wrong. You hit every single red traffic light, the computer deletes all of your most important files, you run out of coffee, the boiler breaks, and you have a fight with your partner over who drank the last of the milk. It's a real stinker!

What thoughts run through your head when it's all over?

A pessimistic thinker will assume that this is a "typical me," kind of day. By default, they assume that life is out to get them. That for whatever reason, life has and will always be this way. They're just unlucky. They've been dealt a bad hand. It sucks. They're stuck. The world moves on.

Permanence is a classic pessimistic outlook. It keeps the thinker from trying to break the cycle. There is a reason for this. It's your brain's way of trying to keep you safe. It's comfortable and familiar, even if it is frustrating to always feel like one of life's losers. As a result, the pessimist tends to miss opportunities for growth, even when they are staring them in the face.

Pessimists also take ownership for their misfortune and that includes things that are completely out of their control! Did they cause the traffic lights to turn red? No. Did they cause the files to be wiped from their computer? No. Yet pessimists will readily take the blame. They'll think to themselves, "If only I had set off earlier," and "I should have bought a better laptop."

Even if we buy into those reasons being true, the problem is they're coming from a place of hindsight. It's backwards thinking. They're looking into the past and regretfully asking "what if?" How helpful is that really? Not very much because it changes nothing. It doesn't encourage growth and unless the pessimist chooses to see the event as a lesson and take proactive action to avoid it in the future, it will happen again.

How do you think they feel as their head hits the pillow? They're probably stressed out, exhausted, frustrated, blaming themselves and full of anxiety about the day ahead.

On the other hand, an optimistic thinker will see the day for what it was, a bad day. There's a misconception that optimists always see the world through rose-tinted glasses. That isn't the case. What they do well is see the opportunities available. For example, while to many being stuck in traffic is frustrating, the optimists will see it as an opportunity to listen to more of their favourite podcast or to blast out their favourite music and soak up the additional endorphins Carpool Karaoke style.

They'll accept that there are things that are out of their control. There's no way they could have known the boiler was going to break, or the computer would crash. Instead of blaming themselves and looking back in annoyance, they'll look at how to prevent a repeat. Better still, they'll look for a solution by asking, "How?" instead of, "Why?"

With that in mind, optimistic thinkers are excellent at taking responsibility for their own happiness.

This bonus exercise is what I get all of my paying clients to do and they love it. It's called the Three Good Things Challenge. Each day for seven days, write down three good things that happened to you and why they happened. The why is the most important part. It isn't enough to say, "it just did," you need to take ownership. Here are some examples:

"Today I enjoyed walking my dog in the park. This happened because I chose to spend time outside with my fur baby. I value their health and I love spending time in nature."

"Today I gave a presentation at work and it went well. This happened because I decided to embrace the opportunity, put my nerves aside and even told a joke."

Over the week you build a record of achievement based on all of the things that made you happy. What's more, you have evidence that you created that happiness for yourself. You start to identify yourself as the creator of your own joy and as a person who succeeds. Remember how your brain loves patterns? As you grow your achievement list, your brain will seek out more and more evidence that you are an achiever. As a result, you start to become aware of an incredible amount of new opportunities.

Can you see how this type of thinking pattern can benefit you?

Success and stress do not have to be related. With the right mindset, resilience and optimism, you can have one without the other. I'm living proof of that. And I owe it all to that curious little French Bulldog, my four-legged hero, without whom I would never have turned my life around. It's funny how life works, isn't it?

ABOUT THE AUTHOR

CASSIE MORRIS-DALTON

Cassie Morris-Dalton (better known as The Girl Means Business) is a business consultant for coaches looking to dominate the online space with premium evergreen programs, founder of the Like a Rebel™ brand and host of the Boss Like A Rebel Podcast.

With qualifications in Positive Psychology from the University of Pennsylvania, Executive Coaching from Cambridge University and MBA Psychology (in progress), Cassie specialises in helping coaches harness the power of a positive mindset, as well as developing their skills and business know-how to stand out in a crowded online market.

She has been featured in media outlets, including Fox News, as the "go to consultant for coaches looking to ignite their income and maximise their impact."

Cassie lives with her French Bulldog Henry where she enjoys playing the ukulele. Fun Fact: Cassie performed with the George Formby Society for the Queen's 92nd Birthday Party at the Royal Albert Hall.

Website: https://www.thegirlmeansbusiness.co.uk

6

LEIGH DANIEL

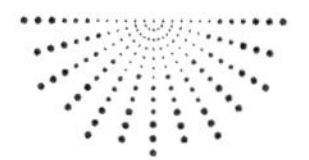

DUSTY ROADS AND DAYDREAMS

I kicked the rock in front of me and watched it soar across the road. When I was growing up, the unpaved dusty roads provided me a place to dream of the perfect life I saw modeled on television. I could imagine traveling far away from the small town where I lived to big cities or sandy beaches. I loved to imagine myself in stylish clothes instead of the ones my mom brought home from the Dollar Store. Alone on those dirt roads, I could be famous, confident, happy, and most importantly, safe. Now I credit my success to the daydreams that filled my head when I was a child and preteen. When I speak to other young adults, I tell them to spend time with their dreams. I tell them, time spent daydreaming is key to creating a life you love. Keep your focus on the life you want rather than being stuck in thoughts about what you don't want. In some cases, this means suspending reality beyond the life you are living. Like I did.

I was a shy little girl. Very small for my age. Which made me the perfect prey for my older cousins. I realize now, they must have been exposed to pornography or sexual abuse themselves. Otherwise, why would they want me to play "prostitute"? At five years old, my older male cousin demanded that I strip with my female cousin. He wanted us to get on the pool table and dance naked. I remember feeling ashamed and crying. Begging. They assured me I would be punished if I didn't do as they wanted. While I stood there under the harsh lights of the pool table, I heard my mother and my aunt come down the stairs. My Mom jerked me off the table and began to spank me. I tried to tell her that it was their idea. But she didn't listen. It would be the last time I tried to tell her what was happening to me.

As an attorney who deals with children who have been sexually abused, I know all the signs were evident. I had nightmares, I wet myself, I was afraid of my shadow and easily startled. I pled with her not to make me go to my cousin's house. She finally agreed to let me go to preschool instead, where every afternoon I would wet my pants rather than tell anyone I had to go to the bathroom. I shrank into an even tinier version of myself. My Mom, she did the best she could. She told me many years later how sorry she was that she didn't know any better. I know she didn't. And she was alone. I was adopted as an infant to an eager young mom and a hesitant young dad. When my dad died a few years ago, we were looking for pictures of us together. The pickings were slim. My Mom said, "You know Daddy never wanted kids". Yes, I know. My Dad wasn't keen on having children and since I was the first one, he really didn't want me. He rarely talked to me and spent most of his time complaining to us that we didn't love him. Or that he was going to die young (he lived well into his eighties). I learned later that my father had depression and social anxiety. My Mom would caution me, "Don't upset him". I didn't. I tried to call as little attention to myself as possible.

Unfortunately, that didn't work. I was targeted by a gang of young boys who found it endlessly entertaining to sexually assault me. By second grade, I was pinched, prodded, palmed, groped, and infected. Finally, being the only little white girl with scabies in the school, my teacher caught on that something was happening. I was moved to different classes and the boys, I was told, were reprimanded. Was it what had happened to me with my cousins? Was it because I was a premature baby and was a tiny shy little girl? Was it because my dad never told me he loved me? Why was I the one I picked on? I wish I had someone to talk to. But back in the 1970's no one talked about child sexual abuse in my little town.

My experience as a child led me to sexualize early. As I neared my teen years, I was the girl in my church group who was caught with guys. I didn't realize what I was doing as I flirted with the boys on the church bus. I felt more important when I saw their pants rise. I desired it. I didn't tell my best girl friend that while we were worshiping and singing hymns, I was passing dirty notes to the boys in the church youth group. None of us really knew what we were doing, but it didn't stop us from experimenting. I remember being lectured by the youth minister. He said he and his wife had been watching me and I was going to be visited by the "sins of my mother". I didn't know anything about my biological Mother, but I was sure he wasn't talking about my God-Fearing adopted Mother. He and his wife told me they could see the evil in me. Or something to that effect. At that time, I hadn't had sex but had been into heavy petting. I was a sophomore in high school. Funny thing, I really did love God. I prayed all the time. I was in constant prayer to be loved. I went from one teenage romance to another. I desperately wanted to be accepted.

At the end of the summer before my senior year, I went to a church revival. It was a long, long session with people thrashing about and being "slain" with the spirit. I watched in awe as people ran around the hay-covered floors shouting gibberish. I couldn't wait to get out of there. My best friend and I stopped at the convenience store on the way home from the revival. That's where I met Roger. He was driving a gold Camaro. Dark, handsome, and irresistible as an older man. He was twenty-four to my seventeen years old. He called me over as he rolled down the car window, "What's your name pretty girl?" He may as well have been offering me candy. Even better, attention.

I asked him to take me to the back-to-school dance the following week. Before the dance, he drove up the same dusty roads I used to walk on. He parked his car and he raped me. I did not believe that groping and petting was all I was willing to do. Not believing that I was a virgin. He wanted to finish what he started as I screamed and pounded his back. Kicking and yelling at him to stop. He got off me with a swear and put the car in drive. I wouldn't make it to the school dance. I wish I could tell you that I reported him or even that I told my mom or my best friend. I did neither. I swallowed my shame and didn't say a word. I wouldn't tell anyone what happened until almost a decade later as I watched a film on date rape in law school. That happened to me.

I wish I could tell you that I learned how dangerous it was to play with boys who were just coming into puberty. I wish I could tell you something different. But I can't. The next few years were filled with shame, guilt, and sex. I was ostracized by my youth group. I was an embarrassment to my best friends. But I couldn't stop. I was a hot commodity and soon had the reputation to go with it. I was ridiculed by boys who had sex with me. I remember once being asked at a bar, "What does it feel like to have had sex with all of us?". I went away to college and had a much bigger pool of men and made the most of it. My promiscuity continued throughout college and law school. So, when did it stop?

You may be wondering, when does the light come on? It started with the realization of what had happened to me. I sought counseling and began to see why I acted the way I did. It didn't end immediately but I could at least understand why I kept treating myself with such disrespect. While your story may not consist of sexual abuse, rape or a mentally ill absent father or of feeling small and helpless, it will seem just as dark to you. Feelings of not good enough, shame, and guilt are painful no matter where they originate. **The first step is to recognize where you are and why you got there.**

I was in therapy for many years before I grasped where codependence and love addiction came from. I was forever chasing someone to love me. It didn't matter how they treated me. Or what they said to me. I just wanted to be loved. Relationship after relationship. I kept seeking validation outside of me. In the beginning, all of my validation was because I was pretty or sexy. I recall my first boss when I was a law clerk saying, "When are you going to sleep with me?". I said, "Never, you're my boss"! He laughed and said, "You're fired!". Or when the Judge called me out in the Courtroom, "Why are you practicing law Leigh?" You are pretty enough to be a doctor's second wife". I was humiliated by the laughter of the male attorneys in the room. I was passed over and wasn't taken seriously because of my looks. But what they didn't realize, was that under the blonde hair and tan skin, I was a great litigator.

I had a unique gift to see people where they were and to show them compassion. Free of judgment. I was quick on my feet and was a fighter. I fought for my clients and became a highly sought-after attorney. I had so much of what I had dreamt of. I was successful and had closets full of stylish clothes. I traveled all over the world. I had a home on the river and a townhouse at the beach. I should have been happy. Right? I could do or have almost anything I wanted. But it wasn't enough. By this time, I had finished with therapy but was still on the path to finding peace and a sense of worth that none of the money in the world could give me.

I stumbled on a class by Mike Dooley by accident. I listened to an audio book and when a chance came to go one of his seminars, I booked my trip. I'll admit, when I got there, I was out of my element with the crowd assembled in Seattle. I wasn't sure this was for me. I sat in the conference playing on my IPad until the second day. Mike said something that I will never forget. He said, "You can just decide to be happy". Wait a minute. I looked up at him as he went on to say, "You can keep going to therapy, or taking pills, or blaming your parents or your past". Check, check, check. "Or you can decide you are going to be happy". I don't remember what else he said that day. I went back to my room and lay on the bed just letting that idea ruminate within me. I can decide. I can decide. I felt like Alice walking through Wonderland. Dorothy waking up to Oz. I was stunned by this simple concept.

I made my decision. I decided to be happy. When I returned to my law office on Monday, I called my staff in the room. I said to them, "We are going to be a law firm based on love and kindness". They said, "We are going to go broke!". But we didn't. What happened instead was that I changed the way I viewed every aspect of my life. I looked at all the things that had happened as gifts along the journey. I used the pain I had been through to help other people. I began to speak to others about my life with confidence instead of shame. I sifted through the guilt and humiliation to find the gold.

A year or so later, I was in my office with a 12-year-old girl who had been having sex with her brother. Her mom was in the dark and when Dad came back from his military deployment, he discovered the kids. The child was shy, overweight, and completely devastated to learn she had to be separated from her brother. In a meeting to talk about it, she sat across from my desk and asked, "Am I bad?" She stuttered, "am I bad because of what I did with my brother?". My heart burst open as I saw the opportunity to use my experience to help her. I said, "No, you aren't bad! You are going to grow up to be the kindest, most compassionate woman. You will be able to help so many people because you won't judge them. You will have the gift of having been through something really hard and making it through." She was crying. I waited until she left, and I was crying too.

My predictions for her were what was true for me. **Even the darkest nights have a lesson for us.** I began to see how powerful my story was for other people. I embraced my ability as a natural leader and began to speak to people locally and on Mike Dooley's stage. Soon I began to host my own events in Key West, Florida. I was always on the verge of tears because I found such beauty around me. I felt love for myself and for everyone around me. The yearning for attention and love no longer consumed me. Instead, I was desperate to give back to the world. I formed, "Project Positive Change" an online community for heart centered entrepreneurs. I created a seven-figure law firm by using the law of attraction and the principles that Mike Dooley taught me. I began to speak and host events all over the world to include Morocco, Brussels, the UK, Amsterdam, and Milan. My latest endeavour includes an event venue in New Market, Alabama. Leigh Acres. My goal is to create an inclusive place for people from all walks of life to feel accepted and loved. My law firm is still based on the principles of love. It causes one of the lawyers in town to chant, "Happy, Happy, Happy" to me while asking me if I want to hold hands and sing Kumbaya. Another lawyer objected to the Court because I was smiling too much.

I don't care how unconventional I appear. I've managed to have so many of those things I dreamt of and to be genuinely happy. Feelings of not being good enough have come up now and again but they haven't governed my life. I've been able to separate the feelings from the truth. If you have ever felt the dark shadows or heard the tiny voice telling you, "You are not good enough" then face it head on. Only by acknowledging where we are can we move forward. I spent so many years floundering in my pool of misery. I was deathly afraid of facing the truth, but as they say, "the truth will set you free." Once you have a clear idea of the path you are on, find someone who can support you in your growth. You don't have to go it alone. At first, you may feel as if you are fighting a losing battle. But don't give up.

Keep focusing on what you want. I realize it can be difficult if you've never had it, but if you set your intention on a brighter tomorrow you will get there. Start by finding meaning in what's held you back in the past. How can you use this experience to help others? I recently heard a quote credited to Zig Ziglar, "You can have anything you want in life as long as you help other people get what they want." Helping others was key to my digging out of my own hole. I put aside all of the malingering thoughts and focused on my quest for happiness.

Decide to be happy.

Whether you're on an empty country road, on white sandy beaches, or in a hotel room in a strange city—just make the decision. Get to the bottom of why you have been plagued by those feelings of not being good enough. Look at your life truthfully, even if it's painful and hard to accept. Find a supportive counsellor or group of people to help you move through it. Don't let the fear stop you from pushing through. The pain of it all will hurt, but on the other side of it, you can find freedom and happiness. Most importantly, you can find meaning in what happened to you. You can use it to help others become free.

ABOUT THE AUTHOR

LEIGH DANIEL

Leigh Daniel is a serial entrepreneur who runs a seven-figure law firm and helps her clients approach the darkest time of their life from a place of positivity and hope. She helps them achieve their best possible outcome both in and out of litigation. Her heart-based approach to business led her to create Project Positive Change, an international online community of heart centered entrepreneurs with 150 members She has created an event/retreat venue, Leigh Acres, and an art gallery, Gallery 111. She has created multiple successful businesses by focusing on service to the world. She has written three books, is a certified Infinite Possibilities trainer, and has traveled the world speaking and hosting retreats. She's been published in Forbes, Good Housekeeping, The Elephant Journal, and several Divorce publications. She co-hosts a podcast, "This is not Legal Advice, Practical Advice for before, during, or after your divorce."

www.Leighdaniellaw.com
www.LeighAcres.com
www.Gallery1eleven.com

7
LIBBY PARKER

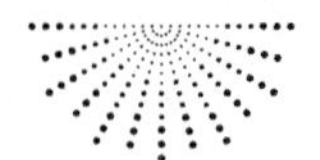

I WROTE MY WAY OUT

It was the Thursday before students came back to school. Panic shot through my body as I opened an email that would change my world. It was sent at 8 pm (why was my boss sending emails at 8 pm?), and said that my contract had not been renewed. I was told to mail in my key & badge of my dream job, never mind that I had personal things at the office and didn't get to say goodbye. It was a cold send-off.

The job had been my status in the community. I had started nearly 3 years earlier when the executive director called and said, "We hear you're the person to go to for eating disorders, when can you start?" I got to create my dream job of working as a college eating disorder dietitian. It had been handed to me, no application necessary.

The concept of me being the go-to wasn't unfounded. I have built my experience and name in the community. Therapists I shared clients with noticed the positive impact I had on their clients. But *this* was the job that made me excited to get up in the morning. I saw the impact I had on the students, I loved my co-workers. I got praise from my superiors.

That email changed everything.

In hindsight, I saw it coming. A new boss had dethroned the predecessor and had managed a team of dietitians working for much less pay than I was making. But it still hurt when I was unceremoniously laid off the week before the students came back for the fall quarter.

Now what?

I won't lie and say I hit rock bottom with no income and no hope, but shame is a powerful emotion.

While I thank G-d for having both a private practice and a husband with a job, it didn't save me from the black hole that I sunk into in the following weeks and months, especially as more details of the lay-off came to the surface.

The rest of the staff found out I wasn't coming back the day before me.

The position was re-posted as full-time at a much lower pay.

And my own, worse,

You are nothing without this job. No one will want to work with you.

Thoughts swirled around my head as I struggled to get out of bed, to have a purpose. While I had dealt with depression before, it was nothing like this.

I did have a few private clients that kept me going, but there was no sign that business was going to get better anytime soon.

One day about a month later, I was scrolling Facebook (you know, as one does) and saw a publishing company I had been following for years was offering group coaching to get your first draft of a non-fiction book written. Like most people, I had wanted to write a book for years but had no idea how. So without any idea where a steady income was coming from I dipped into my savings and paid for coaching. With the help of my coach, we discovered I already had about 20,000 words that we could use as a basis for the book!

Slowly, I felt my passion returning. Several days a week I would take my laptop to a local coffee shop and write for 2 or 3 hours. Between that, and realizing that I gave the same core education to clients time after time, I was able to flush out an entire book in just over 4 months! In less than 8 months, from start to finish, I had a physical book in my hands to sell.

The book, titled, *Permission To Eat: A Practical Guide to Working Yourself Out of an Eating Disorder During College, While Celebrating the Awesomeness That Is You!* It was just the beginning of a total transformation in my business and life. It took the experience of working with all of those college students, and my own eating disorder that had occurred during college, and made it into a tangible way of reaching more people than I ever would have just at that school.

Slowly, I felt a shift in my sense of self-worth. I was able to use the book as a base for speaking gigs, and the premise for an online global support group for eating disorder recovery. People started looking for me and wanting to work with me. I didn't need that other job to serve people.

As I think back on how I had to lose the "dream job" to get to this even better place, I notice a parallel to another part of my story. When I was in college I struggled with a restrictive eating disorder (ED). I remember the feeling of needing to catalogue every morsel that crossed my lips, and would spiral if there was nothing I deemed "healthy" to eat. I chased a lower weight on the scale, even though there was no end goal, it was never low enough for me.

Because of my obsession with food I ended up in the nutrition major, thinking I was going to get a job helping people lose weight. Boy, was I in for a surprise as I learned the intricacies of how the human body works with food to do everything that we do, and how I was hurting myself with what I hadn't known.

Looking back it's funny to me. My ED had to happen so that I could have this knowledge and education to be able to help others not go through what I had. I had to lose my initial beliefs about nutrition to be able to see the evidence-based science of what it really means to be healthy and live authentically, and free myself from the control of ED.

Less than three years after losing the job, I have gone from just me seeing clients in private practice to having four employees and being able to help even more people from so many more locations and walks of life than I would ever have if I was still working at that college.

In fact, many college students from all over the United States come to work with us since that age group is our specialty. I now give talks to campus groups, including sororities, with my signature talk, "give your sister (and yourself) permission to eat." Additionally, I have gone to several colleges to educate campus health staff on eating disorder identification and treatment.

And as I am writing this, I just got the notification that I was approved as a "Certified Eating Disorders Registered Dietitian/Specialist," the highest eating disorder certification a dietitian can get, which took me over 8 years to accomplish.

I don't expect the person who so carelessly tossed me out of that job to ever apologize or acknowledge the pain they caused me, but I can now thank them. Like Elton John, "I'm still standing."

If I was still working for someone else I wouldn't have been able to pivot with the global COVID-19 pandemic and start an online support group for those overcome by an eating disorder that flourished in the isolation of lock-down.

From the demoralizing experience of being forced out of the job that gave me a strong sense of identity, I wrote my way back to believing in what I have to offer. If I only helped one reader, Dayenu, it would have been worth it; but I still get messages every month from readers who share with me how that book has changed their life. That's what it's all about. To be able to impact more people so they don't have to live in the chains of an eating disorder.

You are more than anything. More than your job, weight, sport, grades, address, whatever.

Personally, the most impactful piece came from realizing that I was more than a job title. That it took losing something I thought was amazing to create an even better story. It took a lot of work, and a lot of therapy, but I am finally standing strong in my own being.

You have the ability to create your own outcome. No matter what life has thrown at you, you get to decide how you react to it. It would have been easy to stay in my pity party in bed, but that wouldn't have allowed me to not only help so many people, but to get my own groove back. In the immortal words of Lin Manuel-Miranda (Hamilton), "I wrote my way out." How are you going to react to the loss of an identity? Let it immobilize you, or rise like a phoenix and learn from it? The choice is yours.

Affirmations:
I'm still standing.
Still, I rise.
Nevertheless, she persisted.
I have the ability to create my outcome.
I am in charge of how I react.
Someone has to succeed, it may as well be me.

ABOUT THE AUTHOR

LIBBY PARKER, MS, RD, CDN, CEDRD

Libby Parker, MS, RD, CDN, CEDRD, helps people recover from eating disorders as a Registered Dietitian. She assists them in making peace with food and their body so that they can live a life free of obsessing about what they are going to eat, and live with confidence. She has been working as an eating disorder dietitian since 2012, and now runs a virtual group practice. Her debut book, *Permission To Eat* has helped countless readers on their journey to recovery, and inspired her online support group, Permission To Eat with Confidence.

Libby is a New Yorker at heart who currently resides in California with her husband, daughter, and 2 fluffy pups. In her free time she does as much theatre/acting as her schedule will allow.

Website: https://notyouraveragenutritionist.com/

8

HEATHER STEWART

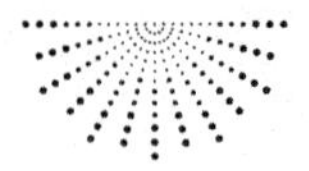

GRIT AND GRACE

"I don't recognize my own daughter," my mother told the psychiatrist as I sat shivering uncontrollably next to her on the sofa, with the doc peering at me over his spectacles, pausing from scribbling on his notepad, ballpoint pen suspended a few centimeters above the 8 ½ x 11 page—the perfect cliché. After explaining to the doctor that I was suffering from debilitating anxiety, having regular panic attacks, and spieling off my history of abuse and abandonment, quite concisely I might add, I was diagnosed with a panic disorder, and prescribed anti-anxiety medication. It was July 2018. Thus began my journey to overcome anxiety.

Here's a little bit about my story...

With most stories, we would start at the beginning. As this isn't your traditional fairytale, we will skip the ideal plot blueprint, and we'll start with the twist, the greatest adversity that I have endured thus far: my first husband. We'll call him Tim.

Once upon a time....

I first met Tim when I was 17. He immediately caught my eye. With his dashing good looks and wide, open smile. His charm, his charisma and outgoing nature—basically the opposite of my shy, reserved, and awkward teenage self. I was captivated. I fell...hard.

We became each other's entire world with reckless abandon. We broke every boundary our parents set. We went to different high schools on opposite ends of town, but we took every opportunity to just be together at any cost. It was like we couldn't breathe without one another. After a few tumultuous years, we married at 21, against the better judgment of both of our parents. (Mom and Dad, you were right!) We had the dream wedding—a horse-drawn carriage, bagpipes echoing off

the mountainside, the works... He enrolled in the Air Force ROTC at the local university, promising that it would help us create the life we dreamed of, even though I knew I never wanted to be a military wife.

The manipulation was subtle at first. It started with snide remarks about my family, which grew into harsh, hateful judgments that I ended up buying into, which ultimately led me to distance myself from them almost completely. This intensified when we moved to a different city over an hour away in our second year of marriage. The same thing happened with my closest friends, who I haven't heard from to this day. In hindsight, now I know he was distancing me from any kind of support system, forcing me to become dependent on him and him alone for support and guidance. That made it easy for him to control and manipulate me.

It was at this point that his behavior changed radically. He became very possessive and controlling. I was not permitted to socialize with friends that I made at my new job. He quit his job to focus on his university courses, forcing me to get a second job to make ends meet. I was burning the candle at both ends, surviving on Ramen noodles and bean burritos, and he was becoming increasingly distant and aggressive. He started spending the night at his friend's house near the university more frequently. The doubt about his fidelity slowly started to creep in. I reassured myself that, "There's no way he would ever cheat on me. He's just working hard to make a good life for us." Girlfriend...listen to your intuition! It always knows the truth! He was, indeed, unfaithful. When I confronted him, I was met with further emotional and psychological abuse. As punishment, he neglected me further, gaslighting me into a corner I couldn't find my way out of.

Why didn't I leave at that point? I was so riddled with self-doubt as a result of his sickeningly skilled manipulation that I didn't trust myself to make decisions. Because I was taught that a good wife stays with her husband no matter what, and that divorce was shameful and should be avoided at all costs. I started escaping from my life in any way that I could—exercise, work, alcohol. I became someone I didn't recognize. I gave so much of my power away, I did what I had to in order to keep the peace, and I had dismally low self-worth. All I craved was to be loved and adored, but I didn't even love and adore myself.

After years of this abuse, neglect, self-betrayal, and infidelity, unfortunately, I was driven to seek comfort from another man. The affair didn't last long because Tim found out, and promptly made my life a living hell. He became physically and sexually abusive. Terrifyingly so.

Did I leave? Again...no! I stayed because he convinced me that I was the one in the wrong, and he threatened to destroy my life—to get me fired from my job and to shame me in front of my family. I confused dependency for love. I convinced myself that the abuse was warranted, that I deserved to be punished, and that I could learn to love him again. Rather than listen to my intuition that was *screaming* at me at this point, I did what was expected of me. I stayed. For a year and a half.

Keep in mind that I didn't tell anyone about what was happening. My family had no idea. They thought we had the perfect marriage. It wasn't until I finally spilled the beans to two of my closest friends that I began to realize that I was being abused and brainwashed. But

I was petrified of him and what he would do to me if I left. I was so visibly depressed that Tim forced me to see a psychiatrist, of his choosing, who confirmed that I was being abused, and I needed to make a choice of whether to stay and seek marriage counseling, or leave and get therapy myself. Of course, when I reported this to Tim, he thought the mental health professional with decades of clinical experience didn't know what they were talking about. How could he ever abuse me? He "loved" me more than anything in the world. I was the one who strayed. He was the innocent victim. Narcissism 101.

Suddenly, the blinders came off. The reality of the situation flooded over me. How could I be so stupid?! So easily taken advantage of?! After a short period of mourning my loss of power and working through the shame and disappointment that I had betrayed myself so deeply, I got to work. I set myself up with an exit plan: my own bank account and my own tiny apartment. Then the hard part came: breaking the news that I wanted a divorce. How it was a shock to Tim is beyond me. I guess I did an excellent job of playing the part of the happy, dutiful wife, while simultaneously suffering in silence. And the Academy Award goes to....moi.

Tim attempted to force me to stay. He slandered and discredited me by telling my family about my affair, while conveniently omitting his own atrocities. I didn't care. If my freedom meant that my family had to believe a half-truth, so be it. They didn't support me, and I felt even further isolated and deflated. But I stood my ground. I couldn't live like this anymore. After 90 days, the divorce was finalized. A year later, I told my family the truth. Of course, they stepped up and apologized for not seeing through the lines. Now my family is one of my greatest support systems.

While I was relieved to get out of that situation, the years of trauma did quite a bit of damage. Looking back, I now see how surviving abuse affected my self-worth on a fundamental level. It instilled subconscious beliefs that I am still working through today. The belief that I don't deserve true happiness. The belief that I can't trust myself to make the right decisions. The belief that I will never be good enough and will always have to settle.

For over a decade, I publicly stayed silent about what had truly happened to me. I suppressed the memories, trying to forget that time of my life like a terrible nightmare. On the outside, I was highly functional—I went back to school to get a Master's degree, changed careers, moved to a foreign country, experienced a healthy, long-term relationship (that didn't ultimately work out), adopted a new faith tradition, bought my first car, paid off my student loans, and started taking better care of myself. On the inside, I was slowly unraveling, experiencing increasing levels of unease and restlessness. Something wasn't right. No, something was very wrong. Nothing held its charm anymore, not even things I once loved.

In 2017, during yet another toxic relationship, this all culminated in debilitating anxiety and depression. I immediately sought out treatment with a psychologist because I no longer knew the woman in the mirror. I was diagnosed with anxiety, began cognitive behavioral therapy, and shortly thereafter resorted to medication.

Traditional talk therapy and medication only took me so far, so I started researching alternative methods of healing. I was surprised, and a bit overwhelmed, by how many resources were readily at my fingertips. I didn't know where to start. I went with the logical first step: Heal the body to heal the mind. I enrolled in the Institute for Integrative Nutrition's Health Coach Training Program with the explicit intention of healing myself.

As I was healing my body, I continued to learn more about the power of the subconscious mind, the effects of emotional trauma, and how many of the beliefs I accepted as truth were, in fact, NOT. After 9 months, I had healed my body enough to come off the medication. That's when the real healing began. We'll call this stage of my quest "the work." The work has included hypnotherapy, NLP, reiki/energy healing, meditation, exercise, EFT Tapping, and more. You name it,

I've tried it. Most importantly, this work has involved uncovering and unraveling the source of the emotional trauma I was experiencing that was the root cause of the debilitating anxiety and panic—namely, my experience with Tim. It is through this work that I have found the most long-lasting and sustainable results. This work is so powerful that I'm proud to report that...

3 years and a lifetime's worth of tissues, pillow screams, and solo dance parties later, I am proudly anxiety-free.

How did I get through it all? Two words: grit and grace.

Grit gives me the steady perseverance to continue to pour into myself like my life depends on it...because it does. Grit is having the resilience to trudge through the mud and the determination to do whatever it takes to meet your goal. It's a deep inner knowing that your desires are possible, no matter how impossible of a situation you seem to be in. Grit has pushed me to not only explore any and all healing modalities, but to also become certified in many of them so that I can serve others using a multitude of techniques.

Grace gives me the self-compassion and forgiveness I need on the most difficult days. It allows me to fully accept and love myself, even when I'm temporarily visiting the darkest corners of the human mind. Grace helps you let go of people, places, and things that no longer serve your highest good. It is the gentle hand on your shoulder telling you, "It's okay. I'm here."

I know that there are so many women (and men!) who have similar stories. Maybe you, dear reader, are one of them. If you are, I am sending so much love and healing your way. You don't have to continue to live like this. I'd love to share some wisdom with you that I have curated along my pursuit of peace. This insight is for anyone who is on a self-development journey, whether you are healing from emotional trauma or not.

Make yourself your number one priority...

...because nobody else will. Putting yourself first is one of the most powerful things you can do. Society wants you to believe this is selfish, but it isn't. When you prioritize your own well-being, your needs, and your desires, that spills over into every single area of your life. Pouring into yourself first will always benefit and be of service to everyone around you. Fill your cup first. Give others the best of you, not the rest of you. To get this message out to as many women as possible, I launched a podcast this year to encourage women to focus on their self-care and to guide them home to themselves.

Believe that you can heal

Your beliefs drive your actions. When you truly believe and feel in your soul that you can overcome any adversity and *thrive*, you will. Believe and trust that you make phenomenal decisions that serve you and your purpose. To help build this belief, start by keeping one small promise to yourself every day. Prove to yourself that you can trust yourself, build your self-confidence, and foster the belief that you have everything you need within you to heal.

Decide that you want a change

There is nothing more powerful than a made-up mind. Decisiveness is a superpower. When you know what you want, and you're willing to do whatever it takes to make it happen, no one can stand in your way. What happened to you is not your fault, but it is 100% your responsibility to work on healing from it.

Get comfortable with being uncomfortable

Vulnerability is the key to change. Sit with yourself and figure out what it is you really want, and then get honest about what is holding you back. Most often, it's the fear of ___ (fill in the blank with your greatest fear). Courage cannot exist without fear. So, decide what you want, allow the fear to be present, and persevere in spite of it. Feel the fear and do it anyway!

Get support

You are not alone. Your experience is not unique. You don't have to walk this path alone. Talk to someone you trust about what is going on with you. The greatest catalyst for my healing has been telling my story, as I have here. Surround yourself with people who lift you up and celebrate your triumphs, and who pull you up when you need it. Cultivate a community around you that nurtures and nourishes you. Clean up your online and social media space to include people that inspire, empower, and educate you.

Do "the work" every day like your life depends on it

Create a daily routine that allows you to check in with yourself. Get curious. Explore. Learn something new every day. Adopt healthy habits for your mind, body, and soul. Invest your time, energy, and resources into your healing. Consistency leads to transformation. One daily habit I strongly encourage at the beginning of your journey is journaling. Journaling is an intentional mindfulness practice of paying attention to the present moment on purpose with kindness and curiosity. It can help you reflect on what is going on in your life, allow you to make conscious choices with your thoughts and actions, and deepen your self-awareness.

Through my own quest to uncover the source of my anxiety, rip it out at its root, and then begin to heal it, I have found my purpose and my true calling as an anxiety and confidence coach. Through my own transformation, which I once believed was impossible, I have accepted the incredible responsibility that I now have to give back and share this wisdom by guiding other women who have suffered similar trauma to do "the work" necessary to heal it and overcome the resulting anxiety, depression, and low self-confidence.

My vision is to use my gifts and experience to fill the gap between traditional talk therapy and true inner healing. I am driven to make a positive impact in the world by inspiring and empowering women to take control of their lives by digging deep into what is truly holding them back. I am here to show them the path towards healing those deep emotional wounds so that they can show up as the confident, unshakeable, unstoppable women they envision themselves to be.

I love seeing women step into the most empowered version of themselves. It lights me up seeing them become the authors of their own lives. It sets my soul on fire when women begin incorporating radical self-love into their lives, empowering themselves to take risks, set boundaries, build healthy and fulfilling relationships, and begin to create the lives they desire from a place of self-acceptance and grace as they chart new territory for themselves and the generations that follow.

Is this work easy? Absolutely not. Healing your mind, body, and soul is the hardest work you will ever do. Especially when you are pushing against social conditioning and the expectations of those closest to you. You will find that most people will hold you accountable to a previous version of yourself that no longer exists. Stay true to yourself. You know who you are. You know what you want. You are powerful, capable, and you have everything you need within you in order to heal.

This is not the well-traveled path. You will experience SO MUCH resistance along the way. There will be moments where you feel completely alone and like you no longer fit in where you used to. Stay the course. Allow your heart and your intuition to be your compass. They will never guide you astray.

There is hope, my love. It gets better. Keep going.

ABOUT THE AUTHOR

HEATHER STEWART

Heather Stewart is an anxiety and confidence coach who works with women who are struggling with anxiety and low self-confidence. She guides them to overcome anxiety and gain unshakeable confidence so that they can show up powerfully and create the lives that they desire. As a professionally trained educator and health coach, Heather takes a holistic approach to healing, providing customized programs and a variety of healing modalities for her clients to maximize their results and guarantee their transformation. She has an M.A. in Education and certifications in Integrative Nutrition, Trauma Support Specialist, NLP, Emotional Intelligence, EFT/TFT Tapping, and she's currently pursuing a hypnotherapy certification. She has been featured in ShefNews, on several podcasts, and presented at world-class institutions such as Qatar Foundation.

Heather is from Denver Colorado, USA, and she currently lives in Doha, Qatar. She spends her free time traveling, exploring the outdoors, reading, and volunteering in educational, environmental, and animal welfare initiatives.

Instagram:
https://www.instagram.com/_heather.stewart/

9

BRIGID HOLDER

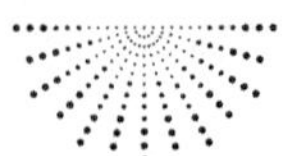

FINDING MY PURPOSE....

My mini breakdown in 2016 revealed in its brutally swift way, that my inner life was utterly unfulfilled.

My mum's heart attack, and the feelings of visceral mortality that came with it, brought my bite-sized breakdown to the surface. Bubbling up were all the feelings I had been shoving down for years. Shameful feelings about motherhood. Honestly: I did not enjoy it. I loved my children, but parenting was not a gig I loved, liked, or was even sure I wanted.

I had no choice but to admit this seemingly sad truth to myself, my husband and to various therapists. One thing my husband suggested helped reveal something I wanted desperately- to be of service to others in a more significant way. He suggested I list everything I wanted for myself, for our businesses, and for my life.

Lists are something I understand because I'm a businesswoman at my core. Right there, in black and white, I could see that I wanted to create an impact and leave a mark on this world. I wanted people to know what they do here, in this one precious life, that it matters. My humble list showed me that my legacy was helping others and four years later I was to learn it was to craft a legacy of their own.

Right then, I realised all my years of service to others were a way of seeking to find my inner self. I joined all the volunteer committees. Always the first to put my hand up to cover anyone's shift or help out at work. I set up and ran many fundraising events and joined others as a participant. Being in service always lit me up!

Yet somehow, until my, what I like to call "mini" breakdown, I didn't realise that I lost my identity in the all-consuming role of motherhood. My breakdown was a breakthrough- it forced me to question what I was doing and why.

I started exploring new outlets, via MLM companies I sought as a source of inclusion, self development and growth. Then joining several online courses with beautiful women and creating a sisterhood, throughout I remained in search. In September 2019, I contributed to a multi-author book. It was probably my worst piece of writing, yet it was the most profound for me personally. After Trailblazers was published, my focus shifted; it was exciting and daunting simultaneously!

With an honest piece of my mind on paper, I could see beyond myself for the first time. I ignored expectations others held for me and those I held for myself. I questioned why expectations existed in the first place. I dared to peek into the hearts and minds of others and find deeper connections between us all. Readers recognised this and started to reach out to me.

My messenger "pings" were frequent after the book launch; I'll share with you just three of the 132 I received over the next six weeks. I occasionally still get messages now from that first published piece, reinforcing the impact and power stories can have when we share them.

"Thank you for sharing your story; I always thought I was the only one. The loneliness I feel since becoming a mother to this perfect angel of a child is unbearable. I will seek help now; you have led the way for me, Brigid."

"You have no idea how much you have just changed my life; I have been sitting in silence and hiding how I felt for three years; I hate this motherhood gig. I told my mother today and she has already arranged for me to speak to the community nurse, and I have had a telephone call with my best friend about it too. Thank you, Brigid; thank you."

"How did your story reach me? I have no idea, but OMG I am so freaking grateful; you have just lit a rocket under me. I have been so bored, so alone, so afraid to say I don't like being a stay at home mum and want to return to work. Now you have granted me this permission—I feel like I got a momma's hall pass, allowing me to speak my truth; thank you Brigid. You have no idea what this means to me."

BOOM! For me, on the receiving end of all these messages, I was like, What the Fuck just happened?? Like a deer in headlights, my eyes were huge, and my heart exploded with gratitude and connection.

If a single one of my stories can create a ripple like this, what could more sharing do?

I wondered, what is it that will allow me to make that impact on a grander scale?

How do I reach more women?

Visionary was the next book, so I decided to share another story. I could reach the hearts and minds of anyone who chose to read the book. Right. So, I crunched the numbers (told you I'm a businesswoman). I wanted to understand how many people I could reach. How many potential minds I could connect with? How many lives my words could potentially change. I didn't want to stop there, either. I wanted positive impacts on future generations, to help heal generational trauma and literally make the world a better place. The figure I came to was staggering.

To get to the seven-figure mark, my goal, I needed to write and share a story every month for the rest of my life. Not only that but hope they all become bestsellers and sell thousands of copies whilst achieving high reading and reviews! The prospect felt too exhausting for one person to accomplish in this lifetime. There had to be another way.

That's when my spirit team kicked in and said, "Well, Brigid, why don't you publish books? That way, you can allow space for many stories to impact the world." It made perfect sense; the ripple effect will be more significant than I alone could achieve. That's when my incessant inquisition began.

I pestered my publisher so much—How do you find the women who want to share their stories? Who is your editing team? Where did you get the book cover done? How did you know what size cover and spine you needed for the paperback? Why did you ask us for a headshot? What does the bio do? How can you sell it for such a low price? Why don't you launch with the paperback, would that not be better?

Many questions, so much enquiring, that my publisher decided to begin a certification program teaching women how to become publishers! Yes!

In October 2020, I officially registered The Art of Grace Publishing House.

By the end of 2021, I will have published 90 stories in multi and solo-authored books. And I could not possibly be prouder of this work! I still contribute to other publisher's multi-author books because I want to reach as many audiences as possible and continue to inspire by sharing. I feel it is kind of addictive and dare you to try!

It's as old as time, as old as language; stories are what bind us. Since the time of sitting around cave fires, stories have given us the opportunity to connect, share history, teach and relate. Stories allow us the opportunity to shape our world. By publishing stories, I have the opportunity to expand the reach of every single tale. To put words in the hands and eyes of people that authors would never otherwise meet in real life.

Even now, after doing this work for a while, when I contribute to a book, the experience is transformative. Somehow writing down each different thought and memory fundamentally changes me. Working through another layer of the onion that is me, Brigid, in the world. Another story peeled back, allowing my true self to appear.

My personal metamorphosis never gets old but what I love even more, is seeing women in our books blossom. I watch them experience having an impact, in the same way I did, that first time I published a story. What I offer them is far more than just publishing. I mentor my authors, help them believe in themselves, allow them to shine! And I'm damn good at it. I'm honoured to hold space for them so they, too, can experience the power and catharsis of published storytelling.

"Borrow my belief until you believe in yourself." I love this quote. I know I have borrowed other people's belief in myself and now I'm grateful it led me to see potential in others. I am here and willing to let you shine your light and highlight your gifts for the world to see. So go ahead and borrow my belief in you until you ultimately believe in yourself. Because eventually, you will.

I earned a nickname after we published INTUITIVE – Knowing Her Truth . It was a USA author who first coined the phrase "The Book Mom." And I live up to it. I'm compassionate with them through their experience; I believe in them, encourage them and give them space to blossom and grow through writing. I wrote about motherhood but now I am a mother to my authors.

It's pretty ironic that I went from writing about hating motherhood to wanting to mother female authors! And now my own children get to see an example of a strong mother who has her own identity apart from them- because this is exactly the same type of life I want them to lead.

You see, what I've learned is that motherhood does not mean being a martyr to your children. It's not sacrificing what you love to play board games, wipe up spilled milk and shuttle kids to activities. This societal expectation of the ideal mother is not true motherhood at all. Being a mother is chasing your own dreams while encouraging others. It's nurturing your gifts while recognising those gifts in up-and-comers. It's feeling proud when you teach something life-altering.

That is true motherhood.

My heart expands on every level when I see the impact I have on my authors and their work. It lights me up. I can help show them new worlds, teach them about possibilities and empower them to be truer versions of themselves.

Leaving a legacy is something I stressed about for many years of my life. I did not want to waste my talents on anything I'm not passionate about. I never knew that all I had to do was close my eyes and ears to societal expectations and listen to my intuition. Now that I'm allowing other people to share their stories, my legacy is right in front of me.

I'd love to digress a bit here and explain how I chose the name for my publishing house, The Art of Grace. Growing up, I had the privilege of having my Nan and Grandad live in the same town. I spent a lot of time with them and have fond memories of mandarins, strawberries and glorious flowers from Grandad's picturesque garden.

One night back then, it felt like I was in a movie scene. It could not possibly be real life. Huddled into the car with my two brothers and little sister, we arrived in darkness at my grandparents house. I remember my mum tucking me into bed, putting on a brave face, whispering everything would be ok, which was not the case for many more years.

The memory still feels surreal, and sometimes I wonder if it happened. I know now that the truth of growing up in a domestic violence household, the stories seem to mesh and intertwine as they were all too frequent. I do remember waking up the following day, to my dear grandfather. He told me no matter what, he would always love my siblings and me. He said that when I grow up, I should never let a man speak to me or treat me the way my father treats my mother.

He brought us into the kitchen to a brilliant breakfast cooked by my Nan. She made such beautiful food, and we were allowed to eat and drink as much lemon cordial as we could swallow at their place. These two humans made such a positive impact on me that when it came time to name my publishing company, it seemed fitting that I use their names to keep them close. Thus, Art and Grace are still making a positive impact on people in this world, leaving a legacy in a way they never imagined.

I wanted to share this here to show you the impact they had on my life but also how their kindness and care continues through this publishing house and into others. Many authors join me because they love the name – a connection I never imagined, a link from the past to a present and a future that I only dreamed possible. I loved coming to the realisation that my grandparents are still a part of me. It's a straightforward way to demonstrate how our energy and love ripples out far beyond our lifetime. Use your life wisely, and you'll live on forever through the lives that you change.

I believe we all have what some call a destiny, a path, a calling, a purpose...Whichever name you choose, we all have one of these. Finding your purpose is a true gift and my advice to anyone reading this is never to stop searching! I have tried many roles and side-hustles, but until I found publishing, I couldn't own it. Now I have the ability to lift other women up – not just the authors I publish but their families, my sister publishers, their networks and beyond. I am helping to build a community that rose directly from the quest to find my life's purpose.

I am the storytelling incubator. Helping others birth their passions and stories into the world—the ultimate creative midwife. And with my intentions to assist the writer, I am also assisting the reader. There is no greater sense of purposefulness than feeling your heart expand as you help others expand theirs.

As I leave you now to ponder your soul, I'd like you to remember three things.

- No matter what, your story matters.
- You can create an impact on a large or small scale - it depends on your desire and purpose in life.
- Never stop searching for what lights you up because the view from that place is extraordinary.

Here's to creating impact, one story at a time!

So, join me and share your story in Dina's books, in mine, or elsewhere. Write! For our stories grant us permission to create our greatest impact and bind us in our humanity.

B xx

ABOUT THE AUTHOR

BRIGID HOLDER

Brigid Holder is a USA Today best-selling author, professional businesswoman and founder of The Art of Grace Publishing House. Before launching her company, Brigid's many roles, both personal and professional, led her to pursue a path of personal development. A wife and mother, she also helms the family business as the Company Director.

Brigid started writing again in 2018 as a cathartic release. Delving deeper into her writing journey, she started to reap the benefits of publishing her own stories and became inspired to help other women do the same. The Art of Grace Publishing House, named after Brigid's beloved grandparents, now serves as a safe space for women to share their stories, express themselves and collaborate to magnify their voices. Publishing both solo and multi author books Brigid nourishes her clients with her mothering ways whilst mentoring them through practical steps to become more visible.

https://brigidholder.com/

10

CANDICE COLGAN

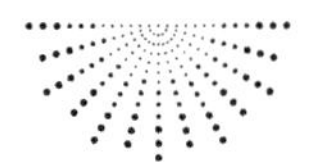

ONE AGAINST THE WORLD

Trauma transforms us. It changes how we see the world, others, and ourselves.

I grew up with trauma. Even though my parents did their best to protect us, we lived in a country that was volatile. I was born in the Philippines, at a time when it was ruled by a man named Ferdinand Marcos who placed the country under Martial Law.

As a child, I knew what it was like to evacuate our home because of a civil war. We ran away to a safe house for some time, ducking under chairs and tables while guns exploded around us. I remember the feeling of returning to our home and seeing it completely peppered in bullets. I watched my parents survey the damage before they quietly, stoically, picked up the pieces to put them all together again.

As a child, I knew the terror of entrapment as nature spiralled out of control. An earthquake shook me out of my schoolwork one afternoon, and I ran out of the school to see the streets ripple like waves. The earthquake collapsed buildings and killed over a thousand people, and I wondered where I could go to stop the world shaking to protect myself.

I knew from a young age that the world could be a very dangerous place. Although our neighbourhood wasn't rough, the poverty within the Philippines meant we had to be extra vigilant with how we lived life and did things. I grew up hearing stories of people we knew who were kidnapped, tortured, and held for ransom. I grew up watching bodyguards trail my school friends to protect them. As a child I knew how important it was to regularly change my routine to derail kidnappers in their intelligence-gathering process. I witnessed a lot of petty crime, including when a man stepped into our car while I sat waiting for my mum, to steal my mum's handbag.

As a teenager, my parents sent me to Australia to pursue further education. I felt a sense of relief at the time as I moved to what I thought would be a safer environment. I went to law school and took up part time work. I made friends and built my life around a community that I loved.

At 19, the one thing that I feared and worked so hard to keep away from me, infiltrated my life. I became a victim of crime.

It was a cool autumn evening, and I needed a break from studying for my exams. I walked out of my apartment and picked up the phone to speak to a friend. I sat in front of a tall building called Casselden Place to chat to my friend. Within minutes, someone grabbed me from behind, a hand covered my eyes, and I felt something sharp against my neck. A cold female voice roared into my ear, 'Give me all your money or I'll slit your throat.'

What ensued was a bloody fight between myself, my assaulter, and two men who were part of her gang. Because I didn't give them what they wanted, they beat me up. Adrenaline coursed through my body as every blow fell, protecting me from pain while my body fought back and went into survival mode. When a stranger broke up the fight, my muggers ran off with whatever cash I had and I was taken to hospital for my injuries.

Eventually the police arrested them but they couldn't prosecute because neither I nor the witnesses to the crime could identify them. I protested because I wasn't given the opportunity to identify the offenders in a line up. Instead, the police showed me a few A4 sheets of paper, with poorly scanned black and white images of various faces. I said no one would be recognisable from this, and the police officer said they understood my concerns but they were sadly bound by protocol. When none of us could correctly identify the perpetrators, the police chose not to prosecute.

A part of me changed then. Even though I knew justice was complicated, I grappled with the weight of it all while recovering from the mugging and assault. I weathered conversations as best as I could, and eventually, I tried to run away by pouring myself into legal work. I became involved in the Australian arm of the Innocence Project where our team worked to free innocent people from prison. I represented people in civil disputes and fought until the parties compromised to stop them from taking the matter to a judge. I went into trials where people yelled their innocence but were nonetheless found guilty. I moved onto public service not long after, supporting people who raised grievances against large corporations and public bodies. I understood how difficult it could be to be heard when the world says otherwise.

Later on, I met and fell in love with a Northern Irish man. We got married and together we had a son. We moved to the UK when our son was 6 months old and my life turned for the worse after we arrived. For the first time in my life, I experienced a community that seemed to not only reject my decisions, but also who I was.

My earliest memory was an evening when I went out with my husband and his family to a restaurant in the north of England. We sat at a table next to another family with young children. Their baby waved at my son, and so I encouraged my son to say hello. The child's mum looked at me, and promptly moved her child away. She made a show of turning her chair so the back of it faced us, and she settled onto her seat with her back turned to us. I laughed the incident off but quietly I wondered if this was how life would be for me in England.

As time went on, I faced one rejection after the other from people outside of my family. A rejection of my decisions, my way of parenting, food choices, my openness with how I was struggling. Doors of friendship closed as I navigated a new culture, and as people yelled 'small eyes!' and 'chang ching chong' at me on the street, I would imagine yelling back a reason to justify my existence. Instead, I knew how foolish and feeble that would be, so I held my tongue and made sure I was home in time to look after my child.

As time went on, I began to question everything I said and every thought I had. I became afraid. I desperately wanted to be accepted. So, I said things I thought people wanted to hear. I changed my behaviour so people would like me. I longed to belong but people kept turning away.

I was broken. Despite the countless times I'd watched the world turn my life upside down, I struggled with being in a community that didn't want any part of me. Every day I questioned my worth. Every day I turned to my faith and cried for help.

While my Australian friends continued to write to me, and several of them flew over to spend time with me, I couldn't reconcile how I could be so loved by them, and yet so unwanted here.

My existence felt redundant.

Social media was my only hope of company during those years. It was a space occupied by people I knew. Even though I had stopped reaching out to people at that point, social media was a space where I felt that, maybe, just maybe, I could be reminded that I wasn't as worthless as I felt.

One Saturday afternoon, I scrolled through Facebook after saying a prayer of sadness. Mid scroll, a graphic a friend put up popped out at me. Against a white background, and in big, beautiful writing, the graphic said, '*Find yourself and be that.*'

The message struck me. It was in direct response to my prayer. It told me that it was okay to find oneself. More importantly, it was okay to *be* oneself.

That afternoon, I realised I had permission to be who I was. So, I began the journey of finding myself.

Later that week, I recalled the activities that I used to enjoy, and I began to do them. I signed up to the gym and started working out with a playful personal trainer. I realised that I could jump, and I could jump high! My workouts became my time to play. I had fun each week and whilst having fun, I discovered that I could do things I could not do before.

I started pushing for more aggressive goals. I started gymnastics, I helped my husband launch a men's underwear business, and I joined a book club where we dove deep into what it meant to be people of faith.

As I pursued activities that gave me life and meaning, I discovered the rules my body adopted because of what I've been through:

In being told that the police couldn't prosecute the people who assaulted me, my body understood that I didn't matter.

In coming to a new community where our differences made me unacceptable, my body understood that I was defective.

Because I didn't matter, I was worthless and inadequate.

Because I didn't belong, I was unlovable.

Trauma transforms us. In finding myself, I had to unlearn the rules my body adopted to cope with the darkness life threw my way.

As I unlearnt these rules, I gave birth to my second child. I started the process of becoming certified as a trauma recovery coach. My eyes began to see people entrenched in unexplainable pain. People who couldn't socialise because they felt inadequate. People who've been accused of crimes, whether intentionally or unintentionally committed. People who've been hurt by religion, whether intentionally or unintentionally caused. People who struggled to find their worth because they'd been told they're worthless. People who society rejected and wanted nothing to do with.

One afternoon in class, I learnt how important it was for the mind and body to work in unity. I practised connecting to my body, so I held my throat with my hands while I softly hummed. I felt the vibrations in my throat, and my humming rang so loudly in my ears that I flinched. My reaction made me realise how much I'd kept my voice low so as not to bring attention to myself. In my pain and rejection, I had muted myself. That afternoon, I knew it was time to stop silencing myself.

I began to embody what I knew all along: I didn't have to be a certain way. I didn't have to live by certain rules or subscribe to certain etiquettes. I turned my mind to God and the people who loved and accepted me, and slowly I found my feet, my voice, and I stopped trying to prove myself worthy of anyone's approval.

Trauma changes us from the inside out. In going through the deepest fires, we face our biggest fears and our greatest strengths. In experiencing the most sorrowful times we meet our deepest pains and our deeper capacity for compassion. Through trauma we find the ability to transform our lives and the lives around us.

Today I have the privilege of coaching people through their deepest trauma. Although we speak about the darkest things, our conversations are redemptive and bright. My clients understand the rules their bodies learn, how these rules turn up in their day to day; and with this knowledge they approach the future more confident and secure.

As someone who's seen crime from the perspective of a victim and a lawyer, I reduce the terror people feel when they find themselves in that space. I walk them through the legal process. I meet them in their pain. I empower them to enter an otherwise scary place informed, empowered, and not alone.

Whether my client is a victim of crime or war, an offender who's trying to rebuild their life, or someone who's committed a social faux pas and had their reputation destroyed, they come to know that horrific events don't define them. They come to understand that their pain and sorrow are just as worthy of healing as everyone else's.

I'll never take for granted the great privilege I have in seeing people find hope in darkness, or the joy in helping trauma survivors take steps to transform their lives to become the person they're made to be – the person they long to be.

Today I am no longer hurt and tied to the past. Instead, I am strong and quietly secure in my identity. Whenever I hear the voice of doubt in my head, the voice is no longer as loud as it used to be. I am becoming the person I want to be.

Life is never the same with trauma. It can cause a tremendous amount of pain. It can also transform lives into something that is powerful, bold, and compelling. If we let it, it will take us from the deepest depths of sadness to heights where peace and the most calming joy can be found.

ABOUT THE AUTHOR

CANDICE COLGAN

Candice Colgan is a trauma recovery coach. As a crime survivor and former lawyer, Candice harnesses the power of acceptance and her knowledge of the criminal legal system to coach people who have been through horrific events, to come out stranger than before. She empowers people to move away from a life of fear and shame, to one where hope and redemption are never too far away.

Candice is also a wife and mother of a cross-cultural family. Having lived in 3 continents, Candice understands the nuances of cross-cultural living and the rejection that can happen when cultural expectations aren't met. She coaches people who have been shunned by their communities, to occupy their space without apology.

Candice has appeared in podcasts including the UK's Foreign Mum Podcast, Australia's Life Together Unscripted, and the Comeback with CK. She lives in the UK with her husband and two children.

Website: www.hurtrecoverycoach.com

11

ANDREW COWIE

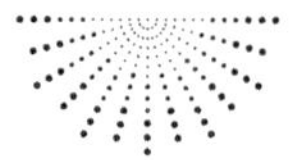

RISE LIKE A PHOENIX

A DECADE ago, my world was in flames and falling apart around me. Burnt out by years of sustained stress, I was physically, mentally and psychologically broken and could see no possible route back towards the light. At my lowest ebb, I was so utterly depleted and devoid of hope that I even contemplated ending my own life. Thankfully the Universe had other ideas and I would ultimately rise from the ashes of this calamity completely reinvigorated. Far from being the end, this was in fact only the beginning of an extraordinary adventure.

At that point in my life, I'd enjoyed a 20-year career in newspaper journalism, working my way up the ladder to the role of Editor and enjoying some fantastic experiences along the way, including interviewing two serving British Prime Ministers – John Major and Gordon Brown – as well as actors, sporting stars and countless other household names of the day. Other highlights included joining the Royal Navy aboard an aircraft carrier in a simulated training exercise in the North Sea, spending a day in the company of a bomb disposal squad, covering high-profile murder and drug-smuggling cases in the High Court as well as the explosive riots at the 2005 G8 Summit in

Auchterarder. Moments like these are the reasons I have no regrets about my former career. I still have some amazing memories from those days and gained invaluable skills and diverse life experiences along the way. Sadly, one day, all the fun came out of it.

It was in 2009 when I first learned that the firm I worked for was fighting for survival. It was a bleak and depressing period for the newspaper industry overall. Sales were plummeting due to the advent of digital media, while advertising – our principal source of revenue – was hemorrhaging because of the recession. Our company directors responded to these threats in the only way they knew how – by wielding their cost-cutting axe at anything with a pulse.

Against all odds, I somehow survived three separate and traumatic rounds of redundancies, but it came at a heavy price in the form of a significant increase in my workload. I suddenly found myself in the unenviable position of trying to produce up to three newspaper titles a week single-handed with only a fraction of the resources enjoyed by my predecessors.

I was working ever-longer hours and under the constant threat of further job losses. The atmosphere was one of 24/7 fights for survival, and I had become jammed in fight-or-flight mode with my body pumping out adrenaline round the clock until its reserves were completely depleted. I began to suffer panic attacks, chest pains, dizzy spells, and loss of all sensation in my arms and legs. On numerous occasions I thought I must surely be suffering a heart attack.

Recurring nightmares about my job were a constant problem, as were nested dreams in which I would dream that I was dreaming – dreams stacked within dreams within dreams like Russian dolls, until it got to the point where I could no longer differentiate between my dreams and reality. But I still soldiered on, kidding myself that maybe one day things would get better... until the inevitable day came when the elastic band snapped entirely.

I will never forget the moment when I suddenly realised that I was no longer even occupying my own body but was floating a few feet overhead, looking down upon myself from above. The experience was accompanied by a mixture of contrasting sensations – relief and a sense of liberation in the knowledge that I had escaped from a physical vessel which I knew had been compromised but tainted by the awareness that what I was experiencing was highly unusual to the point of being potentially undesirable. When I snapped back inside my body there was a strong sense of disappointment and alarm that my temporary freedom from bodily incarceration had been snatched away. In any case, I knew something pretty serious had just happened. It was time to seek help.

After two years of self-denial and attempting to cover-up my illness to protect my job, I finally relented and went to see my GP. The best thing I ever did was admit I needed help. The doctor immediately signed me off work, providing me the breathing space I needed to recover and reevaluate my life. Only once I was removed from the source of my stress was I able to appreciate objectively just how unreasonable and unrealistic were the expectations which had been placed upon me. I was like a car that had been driven with the accelerator rammed to the floor until the engine was completely blown out.

My GP referred me to a psychologist who explained that the symptoms from which I was suffering were what were known as dissociation and depersonalization – the mind's frantic attempts to escape from a damaged body. Like a pilot activating the ejector seat to escape from a fighter plane in freefall, my mind was quite literally trying to bail out before my exhausted body crashed and burned.

The sense of relief at having these things explained to me was to be the first step in removing a crippling weight from my shoulders. Up to this point, I had felt utterly alone and isolated in my condition. Now someone had finally put a name to what I was going through. I was able to research my condition to compare my symptoms with other case histories. The sense of comfort in knowing I wasn't alone was profound.

I embarked on a course of Cognitive Behavioural Therapy (or CBT for short) which made me realise the full extent to which my thoughts had been influencing my emotions and behaviour. Whilst the threats I'd been facing were very real, I came to understand how my condition had also been exacerbated by over-thinking, ruminating endlessly over the past and fretting over a hypothetical future which might never happen. By learning to monitor my thoughts I was gradually able to take greater control of them, with corresponding benefits for my physical state.

Better still was to come. My psychologist referred me to a weekly meditation and mindfulness group designed specifically for people with mood and anxiety issues. Here I met others with stories similar to mine; people experiencing identical symptoms who knew exactly what I was talking about. No longer did I have to endure the blank-faced expressions of people's bewilderment any time I tried to explain my condition. These people *got* it.

These classes proved to be a lifeline and a pivotal turning point. The practice of meditation gave me stability and a firm and sure foundation upon which to build the rest of my recovery. It taught me to live in the present moment and prevented my imagination from running riot. Although I have added many more tools and techniques to my arsenal in the years which have followed, meditation remains the foundation stone underpinning them all.

Its benefits are increasingly backed by hard science. A recent review of 39 studies on mindfulness found that meditation not only benefits depression but also reduces physical pain and anxiety, improves multitasking, sharpens concentration, accelerates cognition, boosts creativity, and increases compassion and emotional control. It can also take many different forms, as I discovered through my weekly classes. As well as mindfulness, I learned Qigong – a form of meditation in motion, similar to Tai Chi – plus body scan meditations, breath work and the curative power of sound involving the use of gongs, tuning forks and Tibetan singing bowls.

Slowly but surely, I began to claw my way back out of the abyss as though scaling a ladder, one rung at a time. Anxiety was gradually replaced by serenity, tension by fluidity, depression by hope, anger by peace and calm. I discovered a state of internal harmony which placed value at a higher level than shallow material gain. Worry dissipated, along with the animosity I had once harboured towards my employers whose cost-cutting I'd initially blamed for my breakdown.

The more I learned, the more fascinated I became by the power of the human mind and its ability to influence the quality of our entire existence. This would drive me to explore the higher levels of meditation taught by the yogis and martial artists of the Orient, as well as western methods of accessing altered states of consciousness, including such techniques as hypnosis and Neuro-Linguistic Programming (NLP). One thing led to another organically as though I was joining the dots in a puzzle. And at every step of the way, the right teachers would appear at the right time to guide my journey to the next level.

I was drawn to the teachings of Indian guru Paramahansa Yogananda (1893-1952), author of the acclaimed *Autobiography Of A Yogi*, and was trained by the organisation he founded, *Self-Realization Fellowship*, in the ancient pranayama breathing technique of kriya yoga, enabling me to access states of deep calm and inner bliss. Then I met world-renowned hypnotist Thom Shillaw, whose ground-breaking conversational hypnosis skills were able to banish the recurring nightmares I'd suffered. Thom showed me how deep-rooted psychological problems, phobias, fears and physical pain could all be alleviated through the power of storytelling.

When we hear stories highlighting how others have conquered suffering, the message is absorbed by our subconscious which works out how to apply the metaphor to our own lives. I began to see how this principle could provide a new and more constructive outlet for my writing talents. If others could benefit from hearing my story, then it would mean my own trauma hadn't been for nothing. That's why books such as this one have such a powerful role to play in raising awareness of mental health issues.

The more I learned, the more I wanted to share my discoveries and use my personal experience to help those fighting their own internal demons. It has become increasingly apparent to me that this knowledge should be shared with *everyone*... particularly now. Few people have emerged from the last decade completely unscathed from the catastrophic effects of the 2008 global financial crisis and its resulting impact on employment and lifestyles. Swingeing job cuts, sweeping austerity measures and the rapid pace of technological change, combined with a global pandemic, uncertainty over Brexit and an increasingly turbulent and unpredictable political landscape, have left a legacy of deep-rooted fear and insecurity and a resulting mental health tsunami. UK employees work some of the longest hours in Europe, and over half of them are in permanent fear for their jobs.

Thankfully there is hope amidst all this doom and gloom. Sometimes a traumatic tearing down of old dysfunctional systems and institutions is necessary to clear the way for authentic lasting change. Even during the turbulent events of the Covid-19 pandemic, we've seen the seeds of a new and better world planted through the selfless actions of the millions of key workers who've risked their own lives and health to keep the world running throughout an unprecedented global lockdown.

Health care professionals, shop workers and other essential service-providers have gone the extra mile to minimise disruption to our lives, while video-conferencing apps such as Skype and Zoom have enabled us to stay connected with loved ones, reach out to the vulnerable and find new, smarter ways of working. Sometimes it takes a genuine crisis to shake us out of our complacency and force us to consider alternatives to our traditional way of life.

My optimism is fueled by personal experience. Ten years on from my own apocalyptic mental health crisis, I couldn't be happier. My life has been renewed, refreshed, recharged and reinvigorated in every possible way. Having left journalism far behind, I now run my own life coaching and therapy company, using my experiences to help others recover from adversity and achieve their full potential. As part of this transition, I've spent the past decade training under some of the leading spiritual and personal development teachers in the world, including the renowned Indian yogi Sadhguru, motivational coach Tony Robbins and Generative Trance creator Dr Stephen Gilligan, synthesizing all I learned into one overarching system with a myriad of potential therapeutic and self-improvement applications.

The turnaround in my personal fortunes has been so dramatic as to be tantamount to a total rebirth. But in order to be reborn, I first had to allow part of myself to die. I needed to surrender to the process of having my entire world torn asunder so that I could rebuild anew. This is the process our ancestors symbolised through the legend of the phoenix and the reason why I adopted its symbolism for my transformational coaching practice *Phoenix Coaching & Therapy*. As an archetypal icon of death and resurrection, the phoenix represents our innate capacity to regenerate ourselves and produce new life out of the ashes of the old. We all have this capability, even if we haven't realised it yet. It's a transcendent experience, known in the east as yoga and to the western world as alchemy.

The symbolism of the phoenix is as old as time and its influence can be found worldwide. Relatively few people are aware that the supposed "eagle" featured on the Great Seal of the United States was originally intended to be a phoenix, sending out a message of the "New World" (America) arising out of the ashes of the Old (the British Empire). In recent years, this ancient symbol has undergone something of a renaissance in popular culture, thanks in no small measure to the inclusion of Professor Dumbledore's pet phoenix Fawkes in J.K. Rowling's blockbuster Harry Potter franchise. It was also immortalised in the 2014 Eurovision Song Contest winning entry *Rise Like a Phoenix*, by Austrian singer Conchita Wurst, which enjoyed worldwide chart success, becoming a powerful anthem for themes of renewal and personal empowerment.

In mythology, a phoenix dies by bursting into flames before being reborn, arising triumphantly from the ashes of its predecessor. Most of us have at some time undergone a life-altering experience, whether that be depression, burnout, or trauma. Such circumstances often result in a breakdown of old dysfunctional patterns of living and thinking.

When that happens, the breaking down of the old can be hugely traumatic, devastating, and destructive. Like the phoenix bursting dramatically into flames at the end of its life cycle, it can seem like literally the end of the world. And in a sense, it *is*. It's the end of an old world, old ways of thinking and acting, old, outdated methods of living and working and old relationships which no longer serve you.

It could be that you've lost your job, that a marriage or long-standing friendship has ended or that circumstances are forcing you to make a geographical move about which you're uncertain. Such changes are natural sources of anxiety and apprehension. Letting go of the past can be extremely difficult and frequently involves a significant emotional wrench. But sometimes it's unavoidable.

In my own case, it was my old job which had to go. This was no easy decision. I'd been a journalist for twenty years – the whole of my working life – and it was all I knew. To have to change direction at my time of life seemed unthinkable. The risks and dangers involved in a career change seemed to outweigh any potential benefits, causing me to stay in a job which was slowly but surely killing me through stress.

Eventually the realisation hit home that the newspaper industry had changed beyond recognition from the job I'd trained for two decades earlier. Advances in technology, combined with massive changes in the way in which people chose to get their news, meant that print journalists were a dying breed. The choice facing me was simple. I could either stay in a job that was making me ever more ill by the day or get out and do something else with my life.

I chose the latter and it proved to be the best decision I ever made. Walking away was traumatic. My whole world came crashing down. But out of the ashes of the destruction of my old world were laid the foundations of an improved life. The old had to be cleared out to make way for the new. And I've never looked back.

There is an inherent danger in human nature that we tend to cling to the old for the sake of comfort and security – whether that be an old shirt, a job, a habit, or a relationship – but sometimes we must recognise that change is necessary for growth. One of the keys to happiness is to be prepared to let go of everything you think you need. Buddhists refer to this as "freeing oneself from attachments" but it's a concept which can be found echoed throughout all faiths and cultures worldwide.

If you're not getting the results that you want, then take a good look at your life to see if there's some piece of redundant baggage which hasn't been jettisoned. We must have the courage to let go of the past, to allow the old to "die" to clear space for potentially exciting new chapters in our lives. This is the message of the phoenix.

Everyone has the capacity to rise like a phoenix. Will you still suffer setbacks and bad days? Yes, of course, because negative experiences are part and parcel of life and there's no escaping them. We grow and evolve through adversity. But with the right coping skills, you can massively increase your ability to deal with setbacks. You will become more robust and resilient, maintaining a plateau of serenity from which you cease to be buffeted about like a ship in a storm by life's trials and tribulations. Persevere with this process for long enough and something rather magical will start to happen in your life. Trust me. I'm speaking from experience.

ABOUT THE AUTHOR

ANDREW COWIE

Andrew Cowie is a former newspaper journalist and editor-turned-transformational life coach who empowers people to overcome adversity and unleash their full potential. He is the founder of *Phoenix Coaching & Therapy* and its flagship training programme *The Ancient & Mystical Hermetic Order of the Phoenix (AMHOP).* His approach blends ancient spiritual practices, such as yoga, meditation and martial arts, with the latest cutting-edge techniques from the field of modern psychology, creating a truly holistic system with limitless applications. Andrew is a certified life coach, Master Hypnotherapist, body language coach, meditation instructor and Advanced Master NLP Practitioner who has trained under some of the world's leading spiritual gurus and personal development trainers. He is the author of *Rise Like a Phoenix*, an Executive Contributor to *Brainz Magazine* and appeared as a speaker at the 2021 *Real Life Magic Virtual Summit.* He lives in Scotland and works with clients worldwide.

Websites:
www.phoenixcoaching.co.uk
www.amhop.co.uk

12

JENNY VUKOVCAN

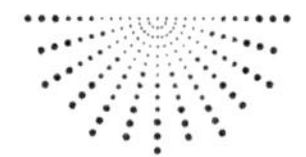

THRIVING THROUGH CHANGE

I remember it as if it was yesterday.

The dreary feeling I had that morning as I woke up in late spring of 2016. A pit in my stomach, heart pounding out of my chest, and sweat dripping down my back. It was like I had a panic attack of sorts. It was hard to breathe, and I couldn't calm my nerves. I could hear the children crying in the other room and my heart sank further. I looked up at the ceiling while listening to the buzz from the computer fan on the desk next to my bed, and I thought to myself, "Is this really it?" "It can't be." "This is not the life I signed up for."

Truthfully, I had felt lost for years. I knew something wasn't right, but I had never been able to put words to my feelings or describe what I felt inside. I just knew that the life I had been living up until that point wasn't mine. It wasn't what I had imagined it to be or even wanted. It was almost as if I was watching myself living someone else's life from the sidelines. I knew that girl well and yet, there was something very unfamiliar with her that I couldn't put my finger on. I remember looking at the ceiling thinking to myself, "what happened to the Jenny I was before?" Jenny who had dreams, a big vision to change the world and make a name for herself. Jenny knew she was born to stand out, create an impact, and make a difference for other people.

Don't get me wrong. I love my children more than anything, and being a mother is the greatest gift I have ever received. Even if I could, I wouldn't change a single thing about my mothering journey. It has shaped me into the woman I am today. Strong, resilient, grateful, loving, and kind. My children are truly my greatest blessings and the loves of my life. And at the same time, the day I became a mom was the day something else inside of me died. At least, that's how it felt at first. My husband and I had tried to have children for a long time, so once we were blessed with 4 happy healthy kids, I was certain my life would be complete. I spent the next few years pouring into them and giving them all the love I had inside. I instinctively knew that my purpose in life was to show others how to love themselves unconditionally and how to uncover their brilliance and honor all parts of themselves. To truly know self-worth at the deepest level.

Although motherhood taught me about deep love and resilience and made me stronger in many ways, becoming a mom was an identity shift I hadn't planned for. This part of the parental journey is often overlooked in parenting books, and I have yet to hear any doctor talk about this at check-ups. Yet, becoming a parent is one of the biggest identity changes there is. You can find information about what to buy, how to baby proof your house, what to do when they are sick, which mommy and me classes to attend, and how your body will change once you stop breastfeeding, but very few talk about the identity shift that takes place when you become a parent, or in my case a mom, and it really should be one of the biggest discussions before and after birth.

Way before I became a mom, I knew I was meant to be an entrepreneur. Growing up, I spent most of my days creating big projects in my mind and making big visions come true. There was always an adventurous part of me that was longing for making a difference and helping people in a meaningful way. I knew deep inside I was meant to make a big impact in the world, but I didn't know how to at the time. I used to sit in my room daydreaming about going to Africa and building wellness centers and teaching women about empowerment and personal fulfillment. Later, this dream grew, and I saw myself making a global impact and supporting women all over the world. I think this was what led me to move to the U.S. in my twenties to pursue a degree in psychology so I could become a therapist and help people create lives they loved. While in school, I found coaching and decided to add coaching and neuro-linguistic programming to my tool belt. The more I learned, the more fascinated I became with the human brain, what shapes our thoughts and behaviors, and how that is tied into the results we have in life. I knew I had found my calling and was so excited to start changing the world one person at a time.

I started my first coaching business in 2006 and loved supporting other people to live their best lives. With every client I coached, I felt I was truly fulfilling my purpose and vision. I got pregnant with my first daughter Emma in 2008, but due to having a difficult pregnancy, I decided to take a break from work so I could focus on my health and new role as a mom. Like with anything in life, I committed to this new mom life one hundred percent and read every parenting book I could get my hands on. I bought all the baby stuff I was recommended to have and was a very hands-on mom. I loved being a mom. I felt I fulfilled my purpose of giving and receiving unconditional love. Shortly after, my second daughter came and 3 years after that, I had my twin boys. Having four children took up most of my time and energy, so I decided to put my coaching career on the back burner indefinitely.

As a mom, I spent all my days giving these four beautiful beings all my love and attention. My days were filled with mommy classes, playdates, excursions, and snuggle time. And I loved all of it. And yet with every playdate, I had this feeling growing inside of me that something was missing in my life. It started as a sting of jealousy when my friends told me about traveling the world or making tons of money doing what they loved, but soon it developed into depression, lack of motivation, and low energy in general. The mom part of me was feeling fulfilled, but this other part of me, the adventurous side, was lacking the excitement that came from living my true potential. All the dreams and hopes I used to have before kids were forgotten about and hidden somewhere deep inside of me to make room for snack time, soccer practices, and school pick-ups. At the time, I was exhausted breastfeeding the twins while taking care of a wild 3-year-old and a sassy 5-year-old, so I pushed all the hopes and dreams of Jenny-Jenny aside and focused as much as I could on keeping the four children as happy and healthy as I could.

While this feeling inside of me grew stronger, I chose to ignore it because I just didn't have the energy to deal with it at the time. Truthfully, I just wanted to sleep and wished for my energy and my life lust to return. I ran myself to the ground both mentally and physically. I started to long for the days when I would wake up feeling excited, happy, and full of dreams again. That morning when I woke up looking at the ceiling wishing I was somewhere else, I knew something had to change. It was my wake-up call to answer my calling and reconnect with my vision again.

I knew I had to return to myself. To Jenny who was determined, resourceful, courageous, and powerful. Jenny, who had visions bigger than the moon. Jenny, who flew across the world at 16 to visit a friend she had only met through letters. Jenny, who declared she was going to move to the U.S. when she was 12. The Jenny who at 27 sold everything she had, hopped on a plane, moved to California to study psychology and graduated with top grades even though she had almost flunked out of high school years before. Jenny who knew that she could surpass every obstacle that came her way because when she set her sights on something and declared it, she would do anything to make it happen. I knew I had to create a change and fulfill that part of my legacy, but I wasn't fully aware of what that would look like at the time. Plus, the guilt I felt for not being the perfect happy mom I had envisioned was eating me up from the inside. I had chosen to become a mom, fighting for it in fact, so why wasn't I feeling fulfilled? Why wasn't being a mother enough? Why couldn't I just be happy that I had a stable family, healthy kids, and an amazing life? Why did I want *more*? The guilt for wanting more was blurring my vision, and it influenced all parts of my life and how I showed up.

It wasn't until much later that I realized that there is nothing wrong with wanting more. There's nothing wrong with having dreams, aspirations, and wanting more money and a better life for yourself. Wanting more just means that there's a part of you that is asking you to *be* more and create something even bigger than what you currently have. It doesn't mean that there is something wrong with you - there's just *more* of you waiting to come *through* you. It's easy to give in to the guilt, the beliefs that are holding you back, and the stories you tell yourself about your worthiness, especially when you haven't fully owned your own brilliance and who you are. You will doubt yourself and listen to others who don't understand your journey. I often heard: "Why do you have kids when you don't even want to be with them?" and "Why isn't the life you have enough?"

As a mom, that's about the worst thing you can hear from someone else. Not only are they speaking into your fears, guilt, and insecurities, but they also invertedly turn your dreams and desires into something shameful. And shame occurs at the identity level, so you make this mean that you are not a good person if you have a desire for more. I took all of it in and made it part of my truth, because I hadn't yet fully owned all of myself. And I waited. And I settled. Yet...I kept hearing this voice inside me begging me to listen. Calling me into my vision and showing me all the possibilities of what could be. Showing me a place where I could take an honest look at my life and finally admit to myself: "Yes, I want more and it's ok."

That morning when I woke up staring at the ceiling, I made a choice. I made a choice to take a leap of faith and believe in myself, my vision, and my possibilities. Shortly after, I started an online school for entrepreneurs where I now work as a Lifestyle Coach and Business Mentor and help online entrepreneurs and visionary leaders discover who they truly are, claim their power, and build businesses and lives they love to wake up to. What I realized was that while I had fulfilled certain aspects of myself as a mother, there were also other parts of me that had been neglected. Much like with any change in life, becoming a mother is a multi-layered shift in identity. Humans are like onions with many different layers of identity, and with every change we experience, a new layer is added. The center of the onion hosts the core traits we were born with. And as we grow older, we learn new skills, behaviors, and adopt new beliefs and ways of being. And as we grow and learn, we also up-level our identity. This identity shift takes place on several levels – our environment, behavior, capabilities, thoughts, and identity. I had dropped most of my "old life" to become a mom. I created a new home environment and baby proofed our house, I went to bed earlier and got up earlier, I stayed home more, I read parenting books, and I learned new skills as a mom. I even changed my beliefs about productivity and achieved time mastery.

What I didn't change was the way I viewed myself. Often when we have one part that is not aligned, it shows up as unfulfillment, lack of inspiration and motivation, frustration and even depression. Being in alignment and owning all parts of ourselves starts with making a choice of who we want to be and acting accordingly. We will always have our core traits that we were born with that are at the center of the onion. But all the layers after that get added as we grow up and learn new skills and ways of being in the world. We learn to adapt to those new ways of being and thinking based on the feedback we receive. We learn to follow the rules, be polite, get good grades, be quiet when others talk, and as a result, others call us polite, smart, and well behaved. Based on that feedback, we form a belief about ourselves that we are smart, polite, and well-behaved people. Therefore, our behaviors influence how we see ourselves and who we are. This means that, in essence, we can create a new identity by deciding who we want to be and align our environment, behaviors, skills, and beliefs according to that new identity.

If you think about it, most of our identity is learned - our behaviors, the roles we have, our habits, how we think, the skills we acquire, the way we live our lives, and what we choose to do every day. Those are all things that change as we grow and encounter new experiences. I evolved and added new layers of my identity as a mom, but I hadn't up-leveled all parts of it. Once I discovered that my identity had been stuck at the level below, I was able to align my current mom identity with the dreams and vision from before and integrate them into this new powerful version of myself. Once I created a new identity that was aligned with all parts of myself, my life, my vision, and my purpose, I felt more empowered, joyful, and fulfilled as a result.

Of course, getting to this point didn't happen by chance. It took me years of digging deep as well as being willing to be wrong, disliked, misunderstood, and looking bad. Those were all prices I was willing to pay to finally get to a place where I could stop, listen, and learn from my own wisdom. And if you find yourself going through a similar up-level change in your life, whether it is becoming a parent, entrepreneur, empty-nester, divorcee, or something different, and you feel like you are not living your full potential or operating from your best self, it will take some digging on your part as well to figure out what is in the gap for you.

A final thought. *Change is a multi-level process of becoming a new version of you.* Change and identity shifts go hand in hand. Every change you go through is an ever-evolving journey to become more of who you were meant to be. The change is about adding new versions of yourself, not subtracting them. It's a calling to step into your full potential and truly own who you are at all levels. It's a beautiful process where you get to let go of old ways and old beliefs that are no longer serving you and create new empowering ways and beliefs that will support the next level of who you will become. You owe it to yourself and the world to be your best self and live your purpose, and that can only come from knowing and owning all of who you are.

ABOUT THE AUTHOR

JENNY VUKOVCAN

Jenny Vukovcan is an international best-selling author, productivity coach, business mentor, executive contributor writer, founder of the Modern Boss Academy and host of the Unstoppable Boss Podcast. Often referred to as the Productivity Queen, Jenny teaches overworked and overwhelmed online entrepreneurs how to manage their time, be more productive, and accomplish their goals, so they can build a business working only four hours a day and have more freedom in their lives. Unlike other coaches who only focus on generic questions and cookie-cutter strategies, Jenny digs deep and focuses on transformation from the inside out.

Using her signature 3 levels of wisdom framework and business freedom formula, she has helped hundreds of online entrepreneurs increase their productivity, manage their time and energy, and build a business and life they love without sacrifice and guilt."

Website: www.themodernboss.com

13

STACY ANN BRYAN

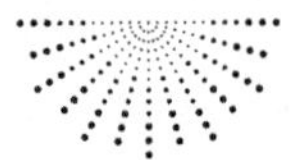

PRESSURE TO BE PERFECT

WHO IS SHE?

The thrash of his hands across my face. As I laid broken on the floor in tears reminded me every day, I was unworthy to be loved, by staying I was choosing. I was just 17 years old when I entered my first abusive relationship. I had watched it all my life growing up, the arguments, blame of two people who loved their children more than each other but stayed because they had so much more to lose. Growing up, through this journey of self-love, imposed pressures of only being able to bring me the facets of what it meant to wear a mask for so long and never take it off. It was remarkable to see myself in the midst of the shadows of lies and deceits that I endured and created when all I ever wanted was to be accepted. I remained invisible to others as it seemed like the better option that way I remained perfect to those looking in.

I blocked myself from feeling loved for many years, the thorns in my side woke me up on many occasions of how disgusted with myself I felt, looking in the mirror at the age of 18 years made me realise everything I ever wanted always came at a fight. Struggling to feel wanted, loved, and hoping for change with patterns of the same scars that made me who I was up to the age of 19 years old. The replay I heard all my life of words from others scarred me to ever think I was good enough, I was too fat, too thin, too black to speak so proper and not light skinned enough to be accepted. These words tormented me all my life and like a thorn it stuck with me for a long time, it was like holding onto a safety blanket as a reminder you are nothing without me.

I feared love because I didn't know how to show it, I feared being loved because I didn't know how to be it for myself. I sabotaged every one of my relationships because I was afraid of the broken parts of me being visible, so I remained invisible. Resentment was my addiction; it was masked by a lack of affection and fear of intimacy to show to others. I was broken inside, and it was hard for others to see. I lacked love to see myself, I abandoned who I was because I honestly didn't know who I was and when I did, I was ashamed of it. My story was not like others, I never had the perfect family and staying was the only option even if the situation was bad.

I held onto relationships afraid everyone would leave, I pushed people away who wanted to stay and wanted to love me all because the words were tormenting to my soul to see myself differently because I didn't know what love was and didn't know how to be me. I controlled every piece of me from my eating, my words, and my heart thinking when I found that love, I would be perfect enough to receive it and he would accept it. At 19 years old I lost all confidence in my partners before it even started because I didn't trust myself and love myself enough to be enough for me. If I was just a little smaller around my waist and a little taller, I would just be perfect. The thing is who could love me, a woman who fed herself with thoughts of feeling suicidal, and the pain that only progressed with fear of never being accepted to herself.

These lies were a part of my life for decades when I spoke of myself but too afraid to speak up for myself facing the truth and understanding the perception of others was only a knife wound, I placed on my own heart. It all started when I was five years old, it was hard to know the difference between what love is and what love wasn't. I always thought having someone love me was hard to fathom as I couldn't see past others without feeling scared to look at myself. I often looked at myself and wondered if I was a little smaller and lighter in my skin complexion maybe I will be white enough to be accepted by my light skin black friends or Caucasian friends and if I was darker maybe I wouldn't be mistaken for being mixed race. Where I fit in within this divided world, it was like being between a rock and concrete floor, it was hard to recognise the difference as I often felt lost in myself because looking in from the outside I could be whoever I wanted, however looking out I was broken, I felt alone and often stigmatised because I never looked or felt like others. My accent was strong, I was a foreigner to many but as a Jamaican in my culture we were one of many I was accepted, my nose was broad, my skin was caramel, my hair was stretched past my shoulders and my arms were broad. It was not until I arrived in the UK that I realised I was no longer a person I was an immigrant. At the age of 6 years old, my voice was meek, and my heart was mild soft enough, shy, and yet strong enough to attain the difference between who I was and who I am...my body started to change at the tender age of 6 years old. I knew then I hated love and the telling thing is this part of my life had shattered me into silence and my trust in others was diminished because I lost myself to other people's needs which scarred me for the rest of my life. I was abandoned and betrayed. The first lesson in learning the truth is sometimes a lie.

I grew up on reggae music, large family gatherings, laughter, and parties, it was my culture to listen to loud music, hustle and play safe because it was the right thing to do, barriers could never be crossed. My dad told me to just study your book, get an education and everything will be fine. I remember doing just that while sitting on a park bench waiting for my friend at Pollards Hill, a predominantly Caucasian area near Streatham, they were known to be led by the National Front, the N.F. they liked to be called, however, I didn't know that at the time. I heard the stories but never paid it any mind.

Sitting there I felt a pull of my hair, everyone loved my hair and always wanted to touch it, as I turned, she looked at me and asked what are you doing here? I said I was waiting for my friend, she muttered under her breath and asked who my friend was. I was so glad when I saw my friend running towards me, as my heart was fluttered with being so frightened, afraid thinking I am not supposed to be here. The woman wore large sovereign rings on her hand, large, looped earrings and her t shirt said white power, I will never forget what she said to my friend, "having n***** dogs as friends makes you a n***** lover" and "not to bring her back here again or else I will tell your mum." I always wondered why my friend always left me at the bus stop when I went to see her and never invited me in, but I knew I never wanted to go back and so be it and so done, I never saw my friend again.

At this time, I learnt that the value of friendship is not by the character of the person but the loyalty of their actions. In secondary school, it became even more evident that mixing was not allowed. It was like I couldn't be friends with white people because the blacks wouldn't like me and if I hanged with too many blacks my white friends would find it too intimidating. The colour of my skin was the scars I wore, and I would be reminded of it for the rest of my life.

As the labels continued, your dunce, stupid, fat, ugly, you will be pregnant at 16 and no baby daddy. I learnt that you cannot accept the values of others when you cannot accept yourself.

I was born in Jamaica, Kingston; amongst the elites they would say. I went to a private school but grew up in a middle-class area of Kingston. My parents knew all too well what ghetto living was and made the best efforts to ensure we were comfortable to never see poverty even though we were living it. My father was born in

Sheffield and raised in Jamaica, St Ann's, and my mother was born in Jamaica, New Kingston. Both wanted the best and sacrificed their lives to give us a life in the UK. Welcome to Great Britain," the loud-speaker screamed, it was my first British Airways flight. My mum dressed me in this white frilly laced dress with red ribbons in my hair, white frilly socks.

The warmth of my mother's soul and her embrace is all she had to define her beauty and who she was. The melting character of her skin always had a soft smile which laid gently on her face, mimicking the purity of her charm and the essence of her soul. But behind her eyes spoke so many sorrows and pain that she left behind when we came to the UK. I grew up in poverty, so I knew all too well how using rocks for a football was, showering from a large tin bucket because there was no running water and eating the little that was there and watching my parents sacrifice what they didn't have to ensure we ate whilst they went to bed hungry.

My favourite place to sit was the window as from there I could see the sky and the stars. This covered me like a blanket, as I knew wherever I was this I would feel safe and out of reach, out of harm's way and out of sight. It was my thing to often wink at every star and pretend they winked back every night. I was invisible to many and preferred it that way as out of sight out of mind. I dressed to never attract attention and stayed away from crowds because of fear of never being accepted and rejected.

I left school with no passing grade, barely scraped through college, and held down a job that I hated. Why? Because it was safe, this was what my mother did, my father did. I didn't want to live the dream of others any more whereby I studied, got a good job, got married and have kids. I was too afraid to voice what I wanted because it wasn't tradition. I didn't understand that because I never spoke up my purpose was always going to be joined because I was not honouring the woman I was becoming. I lived as a victim, played the victim, and attracted victim relationships in friends, families and jobs that required me to follow roles that other people well played to reach success. As a woman this was hard because through my successes I became a victim of my succession, a glass ceiling with nowhere to go but down.

I was afraid to leave this circle I created and by choosing I was losing bit by bit myself, my presence, and my power. The only time I felt good about myself is when I didn't have to look at myself or stand next to someone who was where I wanted to be, so where did that leave me, a blank canvas faced with fears to start over again?

I aspired for love so badly I found myself staying in my relationships with friends, family, partners to belong to something. Looking back, it was hard but a relief when looking forward. To seek change you must be willing to kill your old self and create the new you and the moment I saw my dad gasping for air just to live another day to do just that I knew this was my breakthrough. My chapter of my new me only started when I decided that this pain I invested in for so many years was staying because I was choosing. My marriage became a failure when I broke down from when I saw the pictures in his phone, the texts and phone calls this is when I realised, I felt guilty to give myself happiness and found it easier to give it to others.

No relationship is perfect, I realised after 14 years that I was always alone in my relationship and all I had was myself. What I had to lose, I was afraid to choose myself over fear of losing him, so stayed as I was too afraid to see myself outside of who I was creating, it was then I realised my relationship was built on a foundation wrapped in lack and scarcity, which consistently turned discussions to threats of leaving him only to stay because financially it made sense.

Lies continued. Imagine staying and choosing to stay. I speak on this because what if it didn't make sense, what if it wasn't supposed to and it made more sense to create the happiness you deserve from going within. But I couldn't I use to say, I didn't know how to. I failed in school, I couldn't stay in a job for too long and I am failing as a wife, girlfriend and soon after lost the only thing that could bring me hope for a child. I asked God why you took my child from me, but still no answer replied. I lost all my friends, my heart, my love and became bitter against everyone who had more than I did and what I wanted because I was too afraid to speak to it for myself. Creating a clear mind never meant running from something that I was afraid to face it meant facing the real person from within, who was broken enough to stay with me because deep down she was all I had.

Through this I had many unspoken truths that unwittingly made my future become unwritten because of fear of seeing myself and before I could realise the healing started to chase me. I chased perfection in everything all my life, to be the perfect friend, wife, lover, sister, and daughter. Throughout it all I lost all battles in staying in love, lost my voice staying in love and trespassed the dangers of staying in the wrong love.

You may have heard the phrase "you attract what you are" but have you fully considered what it means? Throughout my life I wondered why her and not me. I served all the lies that I heard because this is all I knew how to do. Like most people, you probably tend to focus more on what you want and when nothing seems to be going right, you wonder why you keep going through the same things in life. I never had the money to invest in a coach, because I never found someone who looked at me. I felt a coach was only for athletes or people who wanted to be fit and well. Little did I realise that saying this was only the start of another narrative of why I found it so hard to get out of my own way. I was tired, I was drained, I was lost.

What if I didn't have a choice and by staying exactly where I was, I was confirming what I was always feeding myself all my life, the pressure of being perfect, the pressures of being real, the pressures of being me. So, I decided to be the best coach for others, and I had to become that coach for me. For 10 years I dedicated my life to others and through this I grew my business to serve women who deserve better to never settle but to create freedom in their relationships just by being themselves. I never saw this in a coach that aligned with me, so I became that for the women of tomorrow to see themselves through energy and here is why.

Through my story I realised why I was not attracting what I wanted because I wasn't really trying to look within myself to see that all I did was learn from past mistakes and used them to stop myself from creating the future I needed. Through this journey I became a global award-winning relationship coach, featured in magazines and serving women internationally to never give up on themselves and everything they want they can have when they don't act like they deserve better but be better because they deserve so much more.

Unfortunately, knowing what you want is not enough. You need to discover what lies within to attract positive results. I teach women to align their thoughts and feelings with their desires to never compromise their standards for other people's perfection. It's okay not to be perfect but you need to stop letting what you are do more harm than good.

Bad things don't always happen to bad people and being a good person is just not always good enough. Loving yourself is not enough. Having values is not enough. But what I can say is you attract not only what you are but also what you fear, what you feel, and what's on your mind.

If you're afraid of rejection, you might let people walk all over you. If you're not happy with your life or who you are, you might settle for less than you deserve. If you think you think it's too difficult to make your dreams come true, you might never reach your destination. When you see yourself as a feminine woman you feel empowered. But when you accept yourself, you're invincible.

ABOUT THE AUTHOR

STACY ANN BRYAN

Stacy-Ann is an Intuitive Relationship Expert, teaching women how to attract and keep Mr. Right. After her own experience with unsuccessful relationships, losing confidence in herself and attracting love, she realized the deep need for support and change within the relationship industry. She has since created a powerful platform where women can connect, heal, and become who they truly are unleashing their fear and setbacks while re-creating the love they deserve. She is an Intuitive Healer, serving women around the globe to embrace their unique feminine energy. She has transformed her clients' relationships from self-imposed limitations, to rediscover themselves, attract the right connections, and empower them in the process. Recently awarded a Global Award as a Relationship Expert and a top entrepreneur as an influential leader accomplished in the areas of sustainability and mental health. She is the Founder and Director of Just Be Solutions coaching services in London.

Website: https://stacyannbryan.com/

14

EVA GRUBER

MY SAGE AND I

In my favourite childhood picture I am 4 years old. My beloved dad is putting his arm around me, holding my little hand. My sister and mum are close to me. I shine! My eyes are clear, curious, and joyful. I show my little teeth while having a big smile. I am present, feeling safe. Everybody loved this tomboy in me. Even I did.

Two years later, my grandma didn't come home one day. She didn't return the next day, and not the day after that. She went missing for 10 days, only to be found under her favourite tree having killed herself.

That day my world turned silent.

Fast forward to the age of 17, I am dramatically eating less. I feel lighter day-by-day. It inspires me to follow my inner voice, telling me "You have failed with letting go! I'll help you get back in control, feeling safe in the end.".

At that time I made myself tiny.

In my early thirties, I am growing my first venture. Commuting between Austria and Switzerland, my restless inner voice pushed me. I ran from 6am yoga classes throughout the packed day in a vibrant start-up scene. By Wednesday my face had turned pale. My energy battery was at its lowest reserve.

In this chapter of my life I felt numb.

I remember that at none of these life experiences did anyone push me to do anything.

It became natural to stay quiet at the age of 6, not to add pain to my family's grief. Moreover, my inner voice intensified, telling me "You should know how things go", "You need to step in", and "Respond to people's needs automatically!".

This way I pleased others. I learnt to say 'yes'.

I gambled with my body and life. I tried to numb my deep sadness and unresolved questions of life, death, and love. I kept my body tiny, not turning into a woman too fast, wishing to feel light and safe like in my childhood picture. I never aimed to kill myself, and my inner voice convinced me that I had things under control, even weighting only 37 kilos.

This way I numbed my restless sadness. I learnt to judge myself.

I curiously launched my entrepreneurial journey. I longed to create impact and be responsible, still stretching my comfort zone. My inner voice cheered, pushing me to make big steps into the unknown.

This way I made it perfect for everyone. I learnt to be limitless.

I am sure you agree we can access more turning points in our lives.

But only if we were connected to our emotions and needs—driven by fear and love. But only if we were not numbing our bodies—through eating disorders and limitlessly hunting for our goals. But only if we were creating more time to access our minds—inviting us to empathize, explore, or innovate curiously and clear-headed.

One of my turning points was reconnecting with my body, and with my emotions.

At the peak of my burnout symptoms, I took a transition year. But I found myself running from A to B again! Luckily, my physical pain scared me off so much that I took action. I intensified my body work - from body therapy, yoga, to African dance.

For once I sensed the true pain. My throat was radiating. The soles of my feet felt on fire. A piercing pain on my forehead interfered with my buzzing mind.

All this tension has been built up and stored in my body since I was 6 years old.

My mind and body felt like two separate parts, as if I had cut its connection below my throat. This blocked any healthy conversation and stopped any supportive responses.

This work helped me to connect my strong mind to my exhausted body.

I labelled my emotions once I became aware of them. By sorting them as driven by fear or love, I finally discovered behavior patterns:

My inner voices are super strong. Who are they? Why do they constantly push me?

I had a burnout, but didn't accept it. Why? I didn't get diagnosed. Running on constant adrenaline, I didn't even get sick.

I turned to one of many of us: I was highly driven, deeply passionate, and limitless.

I didn't go into full burnout as my mind was too strong. As I constantly put the bar higher, I wasn't willing to accept a 'no'. Even while downsizing my team from eight to two, I still pushed it. I still showed up!

This experience didn't give me the credits to take a break.

Even worse, my behavior pattern is among many of us change-makers. Acting as hyper-achievers, controllers, hyper-rationals, or restless, our muscle to set boundaries is weak. Is this true for you too?

Our burnout comes in different packaging. Its impact might even be worse. The recovery might even take longer.

Even years later, I am unlearning bad habits. My brain—used to being restless or pleasing—is rewiring experiences, helping me to respond differently to today's challenges.

The cost of this burnout is high. It is paid for by our "Yes we can!" mentality, lifting too heavy weights, and numbing ourselves. I was even unable to date and accept the interest of men.

Consequently, disregarding my burnout symptoms led to two years of forcefully slowing down. Can you imagine how this felt as a driven entrepreneur?

Draining! Scary! Not me!

I could only engage with one person a day, if at all. Meeting someone felt like sucking out the air of my lungs.

I had to move my body ridiculously slowly at peak stimulation times. Facing any challenge required painful effort.

Fast forward to some years ago, the long-term impact of my burnout is still on my mind. But crucial epiphanies occurred. Reading them might seem logical to you. But being in the midst of stress or pain, who can tell what is good and what is bad? Can you?

Inspired by the book "My body is not an apology", I figured that...

I want peace with my body. I want peace with not understanding certain life experiences, like my grandma's suicide.

I convinced my restless mind to learn to say 'no', stop pleasing others, take too many jobs, and support myself first.

I disguised the 'Stickler' in me, taking away my time, energy, and focus. After decades of aiming for perfectionism, I painfully learnt I need to ask for support. I am not solely responsible. Asking for help is sage behavior.

Gaining clarity through epiphanies is beautiful, and comparably easy. But it takes patience and regular breaks to connect to your needs and wants.

But turning these learnings into action is a different story. It feels hard or overwhelming to take a starter-step.

Luckily, as I was thinking of starting a second venture, another major turning point hit me.

It dawned on me that if I don't get hold of my perfectionism, it will literally kill me! Even if the Stickler stays at its level, it will take most of my time, energy, focus, and joy.

I realized the Stickler can stop me from creating impact. I even feared passing it on to my unborn children.

At that point, a blossoming skill rescued me: I asked for support.

Being coached, I discovered a method which has lastingly impacted my life. A method of helping me to coach people like you to say 'no' to their Sticklers, Hyper-Achievers, Controllers or Pleasers.

Finally, I had tools at hand to face my mind chatter, and unwrap my blind spots.

Within a few months of coaching and in-depth self-study, I painfully discovered this:

I strongly judge myself!

My body and work is constantly fueled by my inner Judge. I named him "He who knows it all!" as his voice was the loudest, coming in first at too many times.

This voice was disguising itself as something good all my life. I took it for granted. Do you too?

I realized the Judge is nourishing other Mental Saboteurs:

The Stickler, making me believe that only if things are perfect, I will be at peace and strive.

The Restless, lying to me that if I pick up all the jobs, I can grow the best.

The Pleaser, lulling me that only if everyone is fine, I did my job.

It felt like a car running over me as I learnt that all my Mental Saboteurs were born in my childhood. They have impacted my mind, behavior, and decision making ever since.

Whenever I didn't feel safe as a child, I took over responsibility. Any doubt, pain, or threat alerted my young mind by asking "How can I survive this?". This question was the sounding board of my soon to grow Mental Saboteurs. It gave them credit for hijacking my mind and behavior, making me feel safe.

Fast forward to being an entrepreneur, it struck me that my ambivert temperament is another playground for my Mental Saboteurs.

As an ambivert, I need to balance my introvert and extrovert needs. But as an entrepreneur, I put myself way too often into "an extrovert's shoes".

I left my comfort zone by giving speeches more often than I wanted. I said 'yes' too fast, pleased to support others. I failed at having decent breaks after an event. Instead I jumped into the driver's seat continuing my fast paced highway, lifting too heavy weights.

I discovered that children learn to mirror or compensate the Mental Saboteurs of their family.

It hit me that I clearly mirror my dad's Mental Saboteurs - especially the Stickler and Pleaser which he himself "inherited". I realized I compensated my mum's by becoming a Restless and even a stronger Pleaser.

Doing so, my Mental Saboteurs found robust soil to grow.

Shockingly, our Mental Saboteurs are all self-made! They find their way to gain new fuel through stress, worry, doubt, guilt, shame, or any negative emotion! What is the dominant emotion in you?

I remember how strong they were at play during my first venture. I am aware of how much I can fuel this fire by being an entrepreneur and coach!

Luckily, my positive mind remained. My true essence—the so-called Sage—never fully disappeared.

Remember the Sage I described for you in the first paragraph? The shining 4 year old, feeling loved and safe?

Now imagine your Sage. It is the core of your being once you were born. It is the personality you see looking at your childhood picture. What can you see?

Unfortunately, too often we only run checking off our to-dos. At too many life stages we push ourselves to make it to the finish line.

In these times, you forget the Sage in you! You even push it aside, not using its inspiring potential.

It is like falling into the sugar trap. If you didn't get refined sugar as a baby, you would feel totally fine and safe. But once you got older, sugar was tempting everywhere. As tears were in your eyes, candy distracted you from pain. Even though it numbed your mind and body, it argued "I am good for you!". Little-by-little your body and mind forgot how life without sugar felt.

Fast forward to some years ago. I finally knew how to make sense of these life experiences.

Can you recall the last time things fell to pieces? My clear-headed mind was in Sage mode, enabling me to energize, be more centered, and take step-by-step.

What did I do?

In all my work I aimed for impact. In my first venture, we enabled youth to deal with their money more responsibly. Now, I wanted to go deeper.

I was ready to unpack our human behavior, and the mindset that drives us.

Being among passionate, hyper-achieving entrepreneurs in innovative communities, I saw the need for a mind-shift. But soon I learnt our patterns are applicable to all of us—to a self-employed mother, a nurse, a manager, or a writer.

My curiosity came in handy. It pulled me to become a habit coach.

A coach that helps you achieve your aspirations, like "I want to feel less stressed." or "I want to be less doubtful".

A coach that supports you in discovering your bad habits, to reduce or break them.

A coach that skills you to create good habits and supportive routines.

A coach that locates your temperament and energy levels to enable a balanced, productive week.

A coach that enables you to make breaks, say 'no', and set healthy boundaries by not jumping on every band-wagon.

To explore the knowledge and experience of a professional habit coach, I joined the Stanford Behavior Design Lab run by one of the leading habit researchers, Professor BJ Fogg PhD.

My studies at Stanford revealed why life can feel so difficult. Why do we fail as we constantly set the bar too high. Why it takes more than motivation to make behavior stick.

I discovered profound methods and easy tools which changed my behavior substantially. Why did it work?

I finally understood how I behave. That it needs some motivation, but especially the ability and a strong prompt to make me act.

I discovered that my Restless and Stickler made me face challenges way too difficult.

I have the skills and tools to make it easier. By taking a tiny starter-step and letting a habit grow at my pace, I anchored in daily micro-breaks sustainably.

My gained knowledge and overall experience merged easily, finally making sense. My numbness was gone. My headspace was back to a decent level. My emotional capacity was strong.

My loops, the ups and downs, the pain and spark, they made me see the bigger picture: I am like a curious anthropologist, discovering myself first, supporting others thereafter.

Still, a bigger piece was missing.

Remember I once asked a coach for support?

Back then, I learnt that my Mental Saboteurs and Sage are the spark for my daily behavior. They make the day grey or shiny.

Within a year I tricked my Mental Saboteurs to become my trainers, boosting my clear-headed Sage. For example, whenever I felt the urge to step in, I labelled my Pleaser. This weakened its credibility. I faced big emotional waves, sobbing my eyes out due to childhood realizations, not fully understanding, or feeling relieved by letting go.

I got trained as a Positive Intelligence Coach.

I envisioned calming people's mind chatter. I saw them letting go of unnecessary survival strategies, which they built as children when feeling unsafe or unloved.

I learned how to get hold of judgment. How to stop pushing yourself constantly, or pulling yourself as an Avoider. How to not put others first automatically, or drown in self-pity.

I learned how to grow your powers by boosting your Sage. To become clear-headed, turning a challenge into an opportunity. Like my clients, I experience day-by-day how I am less stressed, more centered, and respond with more ease.

It's striking that at the core of your positive mind there are... three brain muscles.

You can train these brain muscles to perform better, especially at peak times fueled by stress or doubt.

You build them to live in healthier relationships with your team, clients, and family.

You want them to feel happier.

Imagine your gym or running route. As you train your body muscles, you can train these three brain muscles.

By doing so, you intercept your Mental Saboteurs like the Controller telling excuses as "Without me checking everything, the project will fail."

By activating your Sage power you e.g. empathize, explore, or innovate. By doing so, you turn a mistake into a learning opportunity to e.g. improve your customer support.

You do tiny exercises using your senses to stop the mental self-sabotage. You relax, and stabilize your mind. In this moment you respond to your crying child with a loving voice instead of impatience.

You wrote your own story!

To turn your page, here's what you can do:

Instead of dwelling in pain, stress, or worry, realize that pain is useful. But only as a signal.

If you put your hand on a burning stove, it hurts! Learn to take away your hand. Stop lingering in pain, distracting you.

Instead of feeling self-pity, face the fact that your mind chatter is self-made.

Luckily, you can train your brain. This becomes your turning point, as lasting behavior change needs 80% of brain muscle, and only 20% of insights.

Instead of one-time interventions—which's effects fizzle away soon, leaving you, your team, or HR department frustrated—put your sleeves up, and start an 8+ weeks training.

You can train by yourself, with me as your coach, or among peers.

Instead of not understanding how you feel, assess the intensity of your ten mental saboteurs.

Learn who supports the Judge the most, such as the Hyper-Vigilant, Avoider or Victim in you. Instead of e.g. harshly judging yourself for "Not being good enough!", you start to be kinder to yourself and others.

Instead of constantly lifting heavy weights, reduce your mind chatter or convert bad experiences into gifts.

Like in sports, you might run a sprint but not a marathon if you constantly lift too heavy weights.

Instead of feeling in the midst of fog and weakness, remember who you were as a child.

Start accessing your Sage skills again. By doing so, life becomes more positive and easier.

Instead of being pushed to do something, learn to be pulled again.

A study asked basketballers to score better. Stunningly, the group that simply visualized scoring improved as much as the group that trained physically. Changing your perspective can pull you ahead.

Looking at my childhood picture from when I was 4 years old, one can see that "I shine". And guess what? I shine again, and a little more every day.

Mental self-sabotage is a universal problem. All of us experience mind chatter. Unfortunately, too many suffer from it. My story is intended to create awareness and priority with you. Luckily, as your Mental Saboteurs are self-made, you can unlearn them! You can learn to use your positive, wise mind "in times of crisis".

Are you curious to assess and unmask your Mental Saboteurs?

Are you eager to train your brain muscles and create habits, turning challenges into gifts?

Most importantly, what becomes possible if you calm your mind chatter, and bring more Sage into your life?

I am here to support you!

ABOUT THE AUTHOR

EVA GRUBER

Eva Gruber is a Habit Coach and Mental Fitness Advocate. She supports entrepreneurs, managers, and teams who "have too much on their plate" to manage their time and energy better. How? Through creating supportive routines and habits, and establishing a strong mental fitness practice. As only 1 out of 5 people use their mental potential, this is a game-changer. By training 3 brain muscles and supportive habits, you improve peak performance especially when stressed, live healthier relationships with your team, clients, and family, and feel happier. Eva Gruber founded 2 ventures, and supported hundreds of challenged people. She is trained by and collaborating with leading researchers and experts, like Professor BJ Fogg PhD (Stanford University) or neuroscientist Shirzad Chamine (Positive Intelligence). She has been featured as a keynote speaker at entrepreneurship or wellbeing events, and in top magazines like Brainz. She lives in Vienna/Austria with her French fiance, her yoga mat, and an adventurer's mind.

Webpage: https://evagruber.org/

15

JOANNE MARTIN

BULLYING TO BRILLIANCE: HOW WORKPLACE BULLYING TURNED INTO A PASSION FOR CREATING POSITIVE CHANGE IN THE WORLD

We all have a story! It's that pivotal moment that changed our lives and put us on a new and unexpected trajectory. It's that thing that happened, the thing we never could have expected and the outcome that was a complete curve ball.

I'd spent the best part of 20 years navigating corporate career roundabouts, politics, strategy and everything in between to position myself for success. I'd successfully elevated my career, taken side steps to acquire skills and risen to join the ranks of those who earn a good six figure salary. However, I was tired. Tired of politics, the need to align with the person who had the best chance of surviving the next restructure and tired of dealing with narrow minded people who didn't care about me or anyone else who they worked with.

It's interesting as I reflect on the career I built. There were clear indicators that I was not a fit for the corporate world. Even though these indicators were flashing at me for the better part of 10 years, I ignored them and blazed on regardless. Everyone wanted something from me, from each other and from anyone who would listen. Now that I reflect back, it's clear I wasn't a cultural fit for the cut-throat corporate world. In fact, where I did my best work was working in a small, very autonomous team that offered flexibility to work from home and didn't require huge amounts of energy to be spent on the organisations political minefield.

INDICATOR ONE – I'M NOT A FIT FOR THE CUTTHROAT CORPORATE WORLD

Years ago, I was working in the finance industry and was promoted into a role in a new department. I was excited by the pay rise and to be learning new things about the business. So I got in there and was keen to start proving myself. The reality of this new world was harsh, people didn't like my bubbly personality or attitude, but they tolerated me because I got the work done. Then one day I made the huge mistake of trying to help a client. I picked up an overflow phone call and the caller wanted to speak to someone who was on a long call and asked to hold. After 15 minutes, I suggested that I leave a note on her desk and get her to call straight back when she was finished, so the caller didn't have to wait on the line. The caller took great offence at this and yelled that they would continue to hold. Ok, so they held on that call for another hour.

What happened next was the shocking part. I was called to a meeting with the Head of the Division, I was now being performance managed because of my inflexible and unfriendly approach to clients! Not only that, but everyone in the division also closed ranks and no one would speak to me at all. Not even a "good morning." It was obvious they were trying to freeze me out.

I was in the process of buying my first house, so I wasn't going anywhere and just went to work to get to the house settlement date. Thankfully I also had a successful side hustle I was working on. It was this start-up business that enabled me to buy my first house, as the revenue I earned paid the deposit and legal costs for the house.

At a check-in meeting a few weeks later, I was told that although my performance had improved, they didn't feel it was enough and that 'you should know where this is going'. Oh, I sure did. Exclusion is a form of bullying and the Head of Division and everyone who worked for him was practicing this perfectly. It became really apparent that this was a coordinated bullying campaign, when one day I had a short conversation with one of my colleagues about a task I was working on. I then heard her go back to her team and say 'oh don't worry that's the first time I've spoken to her since we were told not to'.

Boom! Workplace bullying in practice and endorsed by the Division Head and the team managers, who had clearly instructed people not to speak to me. At the time, I was shocked that my attempt to assist a client was met with such poor professional behaviour. My focus was on purchasing my house, staying out of the firing line and keeping my head down until I could leave. In hindsight, my regret is that I didn't escalate the situation to HR and seek assistance in navigating this within the workplace.

My tips for you, if you find yourself in a similar situation are:

- Speak to HR about what you're experiencing (this is something I should have done)
- Contact the Employee Assistance Line (for support)
- Start looking for a new role or consider working for yourself (never let your self confidence be undermined by the narcissistic behaviour of others)
- Create a support network outside of work so you're not going to do it alone (friends, family, community groups, etc.)

Everything worked out well for me, my house settled, and I was free to pursue new opportunities. I understand how easily people can be influenced to exclude others when their own careers and professional standing are at stake. In addition, I secured a fabulous part-time marketing role, working for a progressive manager who taught me a lot about business and navigating the politics of the cutthroat corporate world. He said on my first day on the job 'this is the most cutthroat organisation you'll ever work for' then went about teaching me how to navigate the system.

I developed my side hustle further during this time and took it to new heights. This role was pivotal to my success as an entrepreneur, I learnt a lot about marketing, business and relationships, including how to apply them to my side hustle to create success. I also realised that in any working relationship mutual respect, basic human decency and integrity are critical factors for achieving outcomes and thriving.

INDICATOR TWO – IT'S TIME TO LOOK FOR OPTIONS OUTSIDE THE CUTTHROAT CORPORATE WORLD

After leaving this role, I dabbled in a number of other corporate roles, whilst still expanding my side hustle. I was always searching for what would make me truly happy and achieve the financial freedom I desired. I wasn't quite sure if I could scale my side hustle enough to provide the income level and freedom I desired. So for the ensuing years I still maintained a full-time corporate role and dedicated my weekends to my business.

I was fortunate that during the global financial crisis I had a secure contract role and could pay my mortgage as funds tightened and people were cutting spending (this greatly impacted my side hustle). I even changed roles during this time as I realised my current contract was under threat from continued redundancies and restructures. In my new contract, I learned a lot and was part of a very supportive team of professionals. When the project I was working on ended I moved onto another project and started my true journey to becoming a full-time entrepreneur. I changed the scope of my side hustle to target a different audience group and attracted clients from a wide variety of industries. Life was great. I was learning, evolving and upskilling.

On a beautiful sunny day, I was on the way to work and bumped into someone I knew well in the business world. We were chatting about what good learning and training programs looked like and some of the possible options to land a great outcome. We were joined by my boss at the time, who happened to be walking past. He stopped for a few minutes to chat and we told him what we were discussing. His body language visibly recoiled, I noted this and wondered what was coming next. He said nothing, then left us. I chatted further with my contact before agreeing to chat the following day about the piece of work he needed to deliver. I called him at the agreed time, no for an for answer. So I left it for a few days and called again, still no returned call. In the end, I didn't follow up again and I never heard from this individual again.

I soon realised that my 'boss' had been slandering me within the organisation. He even proactively called someone I was working with and told them to fire me. I was completely shocked by his behaviour and realised it was time to move on to something new. There's no coming back from something like that, which meant the working relationship I had with him was completely broken.

Coincidentally, it was a time in my life when I was ready to have children, I'd spoken to my doctor about this and also about how stressed I was working with someone who was completely bad mouthing me at every opportunity. She advised me to leave my job to reduce my stress levels and also to enhance my chance of becoming pregnant. Financially I needed to work, but from a health perspective I really needed to work. I gave my 4 week's notice, put my head down and tried to stay out of his way until I could exit the building. I found myself a contract job that was close to where I lived and started the next phase of my life.

My side hustle picked up momentum, my contract job was easy and the people I worked with were nice. Everything was looking positive. A few months later I found myself in the city for an appointment. I was walking through the central business district and could feel the heavy energy and vibe of the place. Everyone was wearing a black suit and white shirt, grey suit and white shirt or a navy suit and white shirt. It was depressing to watch. Not one person I saw in the thousands of people that morning in the city looked happy. In fact they all looked unhappy and miserable.

For me that was my real aha moment. I knew I didn't want to be one of those miserable people who was just going through the motions in a job I loathed, existing and on someone else's agenda. So I kicked my side, hustled up a notch, reached out to some old clients and started a new marketing, communications and training arm for my business.

WORKING ON MY MINDSET

Unlike many others who have experienced prolonged workplace bullying, I did not let it prevent me from taking positive action to achieve my dreams. I listened to my doctor and left the high stress job. I took a job to pay the bills that gave me the space to connect with myself and think. I was fortunate enough to become a mother to two creative, intuitive souls. I don't believe this would have been possible had I stayed in my stressful corporate career.

I also proactively worked on my mindset, clearing old paradigms, programs and belief systems. This ensured my mindset was on point, I was motivated, and I was not being held back by my experience of being bullied in the workplace. Whenever self-doubt crept in, I took positive action to deal with that and create my own path to success. I worked hard to come back from the soul-destroying effects of workplace bullying and to create a life I loved. To get you started on your own mindset journey, I've added one of the techniques I use to clear negative beliefs and emotions that are holding me back. I hope this helps you with your own journey to success.

Kickstart your positive mindset work

If you want to start working on your own mindset, I recommend the

following activity. Find a quiet place to sit down and use the following technique to get you started:
Take a deep breath in and out
Take a deep breath in and hold
Now repeat in your mind
'I release all positive and negative emotions with (insert your own thought, belief or feeling here)'
Release your breath.
Repeat this process 3 times for each thought, belief or feeling you need to clear.

Once you have cleared the thoughts, emotions and beliefs that are holding you back, always remember to do a positive fill-up. Here are the steps to follow:
Take a deep breath in and out
Take a deep breath in and hold
Now repeat in your mind
'I'm so happy and grateful for the amazing life I've created for myself and that everything is working out perfectly for me'.
Release your breath.
Repeat this process with your own gratitude statements.

HARNESSING INNOVATIVE THINKING TO CREATE SUCCESS

Like most successful entrepreneurs, my business has evolved and grown through innovative thinking and creativity. I have transformed my business to meet and stay ahead of market trends, proactively adding new offers that are bespoke and fill a niche for consumers around the globe. I'm often told I'm ahead of my time, which is interesting because I feel like I am intuitively guided to what's next in my business.

Working in marketing and communications, I quickly identified that my clients needed something different to position themselves as the go-to expert in their field and create a marketing edge. From my own experience of co-authoring a book, I realised this was a service I needed to offer my entrepreneurial and business clients. Becoming a published author is the secret sauce my clients use to create their own unique selling point, add value for their own clients and build a strong brand.

It was this aha moment that led to the establishment of Golden Earth Publishing, a bespoke publishing house specialising in building brand credibility for creative and innovative global entrepreneurs and small business owners. We utilise brand positioning and marketing techniques to create a brand story that includes a bestselling book. We publish aspiring global leaders across all genres including fiction and non-fiction books, children's books and multi-author books. We help create a ripple effect for future leaders to rise and realise success in all areas of their lives through published literary works.

I'm very committed to providing a global platform for business leaders who are creating positive change in the world to be heard. Writing and publishing a book supports entrepreneurs, innovators and CEOs to up-level their businesses, generate revenue opportunities and magnify their marketing impact. It's an opportunity for rising leaders to tell their stories and transform the lives of others by creating lasting positive change.

WHAT'S NEXT?

I've always been a fearless leader who is happy to walk to the beat of my own drum, believe that there is a better way and try what is perceived as impossible in order to achieve a positive outcome for humanity.

If you're at a crossroads in life, wondering what's next or how you rise from where you are right now creates stillness in your life. Step away from the negativity of mainstream media, turn off your devices and discover who you really are. You may be surprised at what you learn about yourself. Here are my top 10 tips to get you started:

1. Disconnect from everything that is going on around you (it'll still be there tomorrow)
2. Turn off all your devices
3. Connect with the earth, walk barefoot in your yard, on the beach or in a park
4. Tune into your higher guidance
5. Practice improving your mindset (start with the exercise in this chapter)
6. Journal your thoughts, feelings and inspirational ideas
7. Reflect on what's working and what's not
8. Create a plan to take action on one thing that would change your life (remember to take tiny steps with this – what's one thing you can do today that will get you one step closer to that goal)
9. Be grateful for all that you have
10. Be kind to yourself and others

If you start doing this on a regular basis, you'll begin to notice positive changes in your life.

Today is the first day of the rest of your life.

What action are you going to take to create a better life for yourself, your family and humanity?

The most important thing you can do for yourself right now is to get started, kick self-doubt and negative thoughts to the curb and begin your own transformational journey. I understand how hard it can be to step away from the current paradigm and take the path less travelled. However, I firmly believe we all have the power to create our own destiny, to improve our lives and the lives of others. By doing the inner work, personal development and taking positive action you have the ability to transform your own reality.

MY MISSION

As an entrepreneur and publisher, I intuitively know I have the power to create positive change in the world, to help others rise and to be at the centre of the ripple effect that allows people to speak their truth. Empowering others to share their stories and be recognised for the value they bring to humanity is my purpose on the planet.

It's important for all of us now to see the good in others, to help build a positive legacy for future generations and to help others rise. You have the power to rewrite your destiny, to step up and do what's right and to create greater harmony!

I invite you to join me in creating a better world for all of us!

ABOUT THE AUTHOR

JOANNE MARTIN

Joanne Martin is an International Book Writing Coach and Best-Selling Author. She's the CEO and Founder of Golden Earth Publishing, a bespoke publishing house specialising in building brand credibility for creative and innovative entrepreneurs.

Joanne helps create the ripple effect for future leaders to rise and realise success in all areas of their lives. She works globally with authors to share their stories, up-level their businesses, increase revenue opportunities and magnify their marketing impact through published literary works.

As a mother to two energetic and intuitive souls, Joanne is passionate about leaving a legacy for future generations through inspiring children's books. She believes we have a unique opportunity to see our work in action, as we create a better world, for the generations that will come after us.

Joanne is a qualified Energy Healer, has a Master of Adult Education and is an Executive Contributor for Brainz Magazine.

Website: www.jomartin.com

16

MILDA SABIENE

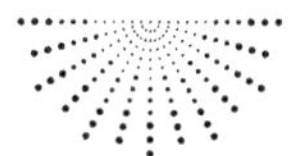

CHANGING THE WORLD IS ABOUT CHANGING YOURSELF

Have you ever felt that you have everything, and, at the same time, you have nothing? You feel so full and so empty. From the outside, it appears you have it all. A great career, a loving family, financial success – you are the woman that everyone wants to be – at least on the outside. But the truth is, behind closed doors, your marriage is falling apart. You have so much anger and resentment building up that you want out – no matter what it costs. Worse than that, your inner self is being destroyed every single day. But… miracles happen. You can create them.

TEARS ON MY PILLOW

October 2008

It was an ordinary day. The kids were asleep. I was lying in my bed staring at the ceiling. My husband was lying next to me reading a book. Everybody was at home at that moment, but I felt so lonely.

I felt desperate.

It was so scary to acknowledge to myself that I was unhappy.

I felt like an empty vessel. And the inner emptiness was killing me. I didn't know what to do. I didn't know how to fill myself up. I didn't know why, while having everything, I felt so unhappy.

I only knew that I felt tired and lonely.

Is this how people feel after 12 years of marriage? Would this be the case for the remaining years of my life? I started counting how many years I wanted to live. I was struck with horror when I understood that I was thinking about a minimum of 48 in my upcoming years. Should I get a divorce?

Divorce was a very scary thing for me. I am from a divorced family. I was a teenager when my parents divorced. I knew very well what kids feel in this situation and how hard it is. When you are in the middle – between your mother and father. When you see their pain and try to protect each of them from it. You are a kid, and you are not responsible for the feelings of your parents, yet you can't do anything. You just want to protect them and protect yourself. So, I swore to myself that I would never divorce, and my kids would not experience what I have experienced.

Stuck. I'm stuck!

I couldn't believe that I had failed! I said to myself that I would be living a different life than my parents, and here we go. I'm like a Xerox machine copy-pasting marriage.

Tears silently rolled on my cheeks and dropped on my pillow.

I hated myself. I hated my husband. I hated the situation.

I wanted my kids to have a happy family, but I wasn't happy. I was angry with my husband and I was blaming him for not providing me with happiness and love. So why should I live with him? I could not pretend any more. I was tired of holding everything together. I was successful in my career, working in top management positions, and always working on something new. I was hyper-competitive, not only at work but at home as well with my husband.

So that night deep in my heart I wished that my husband would get a mistress because then I would be justified in blaming him for everything that was bothering me. I thought that it would be the easiest way out of this cage I was trapped in.

Every day I grew angrier and angrier with him and filled myself with bitterness and hatred.

CRAZY? NOT!

It was hard for me to live with myself, so I started searching for information on how to be a happy woman and how I could help myself.

In one corporate sales training I met a lecturer. After a whole day of training we started talking. And during our discussion, I suggested we could work together to do training for other women on how to be happy. In all honesty, I was searching for training for myself.

So, we agreed that it was possible, and I started organizing the group. In 2009 it was very hard to sell a seminar that was not about business, sales, or marketing. I spoke with many of my friends, inviting them to a special seminar for women – "Happy Woman". But all of them treated me like I was crazy. Because I looked happy to them and they also were sure that they were living a happy life.

When I understood that I would not be able to organize the first seminar in my city, I decided to organize it in another place. And I did it. In this two-day seminar I was crying and crying. I could not say a single word without tears. I needed to let go of all the sadness, resentment, and anger. That was the beginning of my path to knowing myself. I dived deep into my heart during the seminar, I let myself see what I had been hiding so many years from myself and I let myself heal these wounds with love.

This seminar was the start of me organizing seminars and retreats for women. When I came home, I knew that if I did not want to feel alone, I needed to invite my friends to this seminar, so we would be on the same page and they would not think that I'd gone crazy. So, I organized and attended more than 10 seminars and each time I heard something new and found some new details about myself. Also, I benefited because then I had my new tribe of women and we were on the same path – courageous, true to ourselves, supportive and on the way to our happy women's life.

DON'T TEAR YOURSELF APART!

Well, my wish came true as not only did my husband take one mistress, but several.

So, in February 2011 I began the process to divorce my husband. However, after a full year of struggle we still couldn't come to a resolution. Then, to my shock and relief, my husband got one of his mistresses pregnant!

I was finally in a place where my divorce could be justified. Finally, I could be free.

But the happiness didn't last long. Our younger daughter had severe pain in the chest, so we needed to go to the hospital. I was scared. After examining her, the doctor said that it was the stomach's reaction to the stress felt at home. For me that was like a wakeup call.

That year during the Christmas celebrations my granny said something profound to me. She had been married three times, and she told me, *"Milda, stop tearing yourself apart. Stop this divorce. Love yourself, take care of yourself. This is the main thing!"*

Her words touched me deep in my heart. And I understood my pride. I realized that all this time, I hadn't taken responsibility for my life, all this time I had so much knowledge and so much wisdom inside me, but it was only in my mind, I hadn't put any of it into practice.

I reflected on all of my years since 2008. Especially the year 2011. It was a year of struggle when you do and initiate things, but it seems you bounce off the wall. There was no flow, only obstacles and problems that I needed to solve. I understood that I could not do the same things and expect different results. So, I needed to do something that I have never done before. I needed to put my knowledge and wisdom into practice. You know, that it's one thing to know things and the other thing is to do them.

Let's do it!

WHEN MIRACLES HAPPEN

New Year's Eve, 2012

2011 was coming to an end. I was still married. There was a pregnant mistress. Tensions in my relationship with my husband were high. I wanted a new life. But I also understood that being the same old me I could create only the same old world around me. Did I like it? No! I needed to change myself to be with this man. I already understood that I can't change the other person. The only person I can change is me!

So, I committed to the next six months of doing gratitude practice. I knew that it was a very powerful spiritual practice. I needed to test it and to make sure it did really make miracles. And when I'm talking about *gratitude* I'm not talking about *thanking*.

At that time, I already knew and practiced myself that words carry deep meaning and each word has different vibrations. Gratitude is one of the simplest spiritual practices. It is also one of the strongest I know.

I told myself that in the next six months I would do three things:

1. Every time I wanted to say something rude or disgusting to my husband, I would stop myself.

2. I would transform my mind and find something good in the situation.

3. I would loudly proclaim my gratitude to my husband and how grateful I was to him.

It was easy to say! And it was not so easy to do! But I did it.

It was the beginning of another deep transformation for me. It was about changing my habits and reactions – physical, emotional, and mental. I knew that if I wouldn't change it would not matter if I was together with my husband or with another man, I would not be able to create another reality if I would not change myself.

CHANGE WAS JUST ABOUT ME

The experiment started on the first day of January. To change a habit, you need from 90 days to a year and a half. So, I decided that 6 months would be enough for me to change one habit to another. To change my habit of nagging to support and gratefulness for what I have.

The first step was relatively easy for me. It meant just to shut up and say nothing rude.

The second one took a bit more work. I just needed to see something good when usually I was used to blaming and nagging. I noticed that debate started in my head that there was nothing good in this situation. Then I stopped myself saying – "*Milda, come on, you know that there is always something good. Even in the worst situations, you can find something positive and useful.*" It usually took me a few seconds to find what's good in there.

But the third step was incredibly difficult to do. Oh my God, I needed to express my gratitude to my husband loudly! My throat tightened. I could barely make out words. In the beginning, I was just technically stabbing words through my clenched teeth. To say the usual "thank you" would have been so easy, but to say "I am grateful to you for... " was infinitely difficult.

When women in the retreats or individual sessions ask me "*Shouldn't the gratefulness be sincere and come from your heart?*" I answer, yes, it should. But when you don't have such a habit you just need to form it. And if I was waiting until I could do it sincerely, I would have found myself in the grave first. Because at that moment I hated my husband. And when you hate, gratefulness does not come naturally. What comes out naturally and from your heart is nagging, blaming, shaming, sarcasm and all that kind of stuff.

The first month was like training. It was absolutely the same as when you start going to the gym after a very long break and you feel all your muscles again. You just do exercises because you know that after some time your muscles will get stronger, and they will not hurt that much.

My husband didn't know anything about my new experiment. So, the first month he was looking at me suspiciously. Because instead of the usual accusations he received gratitude.

After a month and a half, he said to me "*I absolutely don't understand you!*"

This was the best sign and motivation for me that I was moving in the right direction. I was changing.

Of course, there were moments when I wanted to stop everything because I was frustrated. But the only one thing that inspired and kept me moving forward was that I promised myself and I wanted to change myself.

I was doing this experiment just for me. I wasn't expecting him to change.

The most miraculous thing for me was that after five months my husband started inviting me to go on trips with his co-workers and respectfully introduced me to them as his wife. And he started expressing gratitude to me himself!

And over time, things shifted. Gradually at first, but then with higher intensity. Not only did the relationship between my husband and me get restored, but I gained a much deeper understanding of love and how to love myself.

I also understood that it is possible to move from hatred to respect and then even to love a person again. I experienced everything myself. And I know that everything is possible. This situation was like a wakeup call and a blessing to me.

It inspired me to work with women. I started coaching them individually. Wanting to help more women, I organized women's circles where I helped women understand themselves and how, by changing themselves, they could create an impact on their relationships and marriage. As a result of this there were a lot of happy women and a lot of saved marriages. Later, I started organizing retreats all over the world, coaching men and couples.

I left my corporate job and for more than eight years I have been devoted to coaching people. I help people dive deep inside and understand the mindset of how they can create their world, so that they can connect their business and material life with spirituality in a healthy and prosperous way. And applying a holistic approach thrives in all aspects of life—self-awareness, relationships, and business.

Remember, you create your own world. It's your decision and your choice on how you feel and how you live. Respect yourself and choose wisely. If you need my help, I'm always here.

ABOUT THE AUTHOR

MILDA SABIENE

Milda Sabiene is a business psychologist & holistic coach who works with entrepreneurs who from the outside seems to have it all – great career, family, financial success but deep inside they feel anger, resentment and emptiness building up that they want out – no matter what it costs. She helps them to dive deep inside and understand their mindset how they create their world so that they can connect business and material life with spirituality in healthy and prospering way. And applying holistic approach thrive in all aspects of life – self-awareness, relationships, and business. She launched her business following a decade working at top management positions and for more than 15 years is entrepreneur herself. She is best-selling author in Lithuania "7 Laws of the Universe". She organizes goal setting retreats and retreats for women all over the world.

Website: https://www.mildasabiene.com

17

DR. KRISTINA TICKLER WELSOME

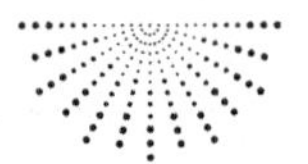

HEALING THE WORLD ONE HEART, MIND, BODY & SOUL AT A TIME

OUR PAIN BECOMES OUR PASSION

So often in life, it is our greatest pain that becomes our passion. At the beginning of my adulthood, while still in college working and taking courses preparing to apply to medical school, I had a serious run in with a drunk driver. It ended my dancing career, made me realize I didn't want to be a physician, and led me to the field of physical therapy. Later in adulthood, the pain of my marriage ending gave me an awareness that I had codependent tendencies and absolutely no self-worth. This led me down the winding path of healing and personal discovery as I learned about self-care, self-compassion, and ultimately self-love. Throughout my life I had learned to silence myself to keep the peace, to not rock the boat in order to please those around me. What seemed most important to me was to make other people happy, and I never really paid attention to my own happiness. Once I realized that healing myself and following my own deepest desires to be happy, was also an investment that paid dividends to those around me, I learned to pay attention to what my desires were and to make sure I expressed them so my voice could be heard.

Change is inevitable. Even if we choose to stay neutral and let the tide carry us, we'll still be swept along and taken somewhere new. Embracing change is critical and tantamount to our success if we want to go in the direction that we choose. We need to be open and willing to change, because that's where personal growth and transformation occurs. It takes us on a journey from point A to point B. And in that process, we gain awareness, experience, knowledge, and skills that shape us into the newer version of yourself. Hopefully a more complete and integrated version who is ready to use their voice and power to create even more positive impact in the world around us.

I've never met a person who hasn't encountered some kind of adversity in their life. Whether it be ancestral, at birth, early childhood, childhood, adolescence, high school, college, young adulthood, adulthood, marriage, the birth or death of a child, midlife, divorce, a committed but unhappy marriage, financial hardship, toxic workplaces, toxic relationships or an unfulfilled life. Unfortunately, pain and suffering are very human conditions that very few of us escape. What's critical is how we let it impact us. Do we let it forge us by fire so we can rise up like a phoenix from the ashes? Do we let the slow, consistent rolling of water create the foundation and bedrock of our river? Do we let that pain be felt and experienced, accepted and surrendered to, so that we don't prolong the suffering by telling ourselves the same awful story over and over again, limiting our ability to grow and change and become the person that pain can shape us into? If we allow that pain to become our passion, it can be the foundation from which we were created and developed, shaping the person we are today.

Once we've walked that path, it is then easy to turn back and offer a helping hand to those who are just one step behind us. To shine a light, show them there's a way forward, offer them a helping hand, to encourage them in their darkest moments and to celebrate when they get to the vista point exposing all the beauty that lies ahead. From a car accident that ended my dancing career but led me down the path of physical therapy, to the end of a quarter century of marriage that left me with a broken heart full of love for three amazing children, to the fear and pain of walking away from a career I spent my life building to follow my heart's calling...the view is nothing but exhilarating. In becoming a change maker you can use the skills and knowledge gained to create the most positive impact in the world that you possibly can. Creating impact is an amazingly empowering feeling - whether you help just one person or you help millions. I implore you to look inside and fearlessly embrace your calling, so that you can overcome whatever adversity you're facing, and be a changemaker who creates a positive impact in the world with your innate gifts.

WHAT THE IMPACT OF EXTERNAL FORCES BRING TO US

There have been forces at play on us our entire lives. Some that we're consciously aware of and some that are simply running in our subconscious. Just as those things can impact us, so too can our own thoughts, words, actions, and behaviors have an impact on the people we come into contact with, whether intentional or unintentional. It's important to be constantly aware and cognizant of what impacts us - our ancestors, family of origin, environment, culture, religion, friends, and loved ones and in turn, how we transform those influences into energy that affects others.

External forces bring us opportunities to hide, to change, to grow. The choice is up to no one but us. We can choose to multiply our past pain and prolong our suffering, or we can surrender to it , release it and focus on multiplying our joy. I choose joy, abundance, mental and physical health, pleasure, and love. I give myself permission for it all! Opportunities, successes, errors, mistakes, missing the mark, getting it wrong- I'm here for it all. I'm going to give myself the opportunity to fail fabulously, but in a forward direction. I'm going to lean into what's right for me. I'm going to give myself permission to take bold action. I'm going to expect failure on the way to my ultimate success. And I'm going to have self-love, compassion, and grace for myself along the way.

What you seek is seeking you. When the time is right and it shows up, go all in. For me, gaining the clarity, connection, appreciation and assistance I desired created relationships and friendships much needed in my life. Learning to ask for the things I need helped me get better at receiving. Being aware and grateful for all that I have in my life allows me to operate from a place of abundance not lack. Serving others has allowed me to gain the beautiful experience of self-confidence, to know that I am ok and not broken, to recognize that I'm no longer sorry for being my authentic self. I know that I can have a greater impact in this world. The success I've had has provided me with awareness and a change of perspective. The failures showed me areas I could improve on. The weak can become strong. Emotional harm can be healed. We can gain freedom and connect to our own sense of self. I never would have gained that skill set if I hadn't gone through the life experiences and the pain that I did.

Whatever it is you want in this life...give it to yourself. Empower yourself to go get it. If you want love - love yourself. If you want money - make money. If you want approval, validation or permission - give it to yourself. The darkest place in your life is when you self-abandon. When you say yes but you really mean no. When you don't show up for yourself. When you don't take care of yourself. When you put others' needs over your own. Reclaim yourself and own your power. You can be, do and have anything you desire. Have the courage to own who you are. As Clarissa Pinkola Estes says in Women Who Run With The Wolves, "You have to howl so your pack knows where you are". Design your life in a way so as to transform people into what they want to be. Surrender your emotions. Ask for help from the divine and the people in your life. Be in relationship with your highest self and those who surround you. . Release the resistance and move forward in the direction of your dreams. Let it be easy. Let it be fun. Let it be miraculous. Let's create an impact. Live your life in a way that lights you up. "If your plan is great enough, there is no pain that's big enough to stop you. Show up as a miracle. Don't look for them to occur for you. " - Danielle Delgado. How good are you willing to let your life become? And how soon?

THE TRANSFORMATION WE CHOOSE TO CREATE WITH THAT IMPACT - HEALING THE WORLD, ONE HEART, MIND, BODY & SOUL AT A TIME

What would you choose to do if you knew you wouldn't fail? Let it be easy. The solution already exists. You may not see it, but on a spiritual level it's already planned and ready for you. We will attract our desires when we are in the right vibrational match. Prepare yourself to be the person who has the capacity to hold abundance and love simultaneously. Be there for yourself so that you can be there for others. We drop into our zone of genius, when we allow and accept our truth. We don't need others to validate us. We can show up for ourselves like no one else ever would, could, or would know how to. So what is the new story that you need to write about yourself - about your past, your present, and the amazing future you're ready to create?

Our pain can become our passion. Our weaknesses can become strengths. We can give ourselves permission to follow our passions and create a life we love.

"The first time you pull away and find power in standing on your own, your heart is marked by the wild" - Brene Brown. You feel yourself welcomed home like the prodigal son and embraced by the divine. You remember the feeling of being real and wild and free. And you recognize that you can never go back to the inauthentic version of yourself or the role you had been playing. The mask of your false self is left on the floor like the detritus of a Venetian Carnival season. It no longer suits you and you revel in the feeling of your own glowing skin. This is when the impacts of the past truly transform you into the best version of your true self.

I was on autopilot, living in survival mode. I let my doubts, fears, and indecision keep me small and hidden. The expectations of others, traditional academic and health care service models, and societal norms limited my aspirations until a little spark of magic called my name. This spark lit up my self-awareness and intuition and allowed me to speak up. The fire built, encouraging me to do things differently, create change, shake things up and make life better for myself and those I serve. I allowed my heart to lead me as I learned to become the change I wanted to see in the world. Life is meant to be a grand adventure, full of joy and pleasure and fun. We are meant to have time to breathe, to feel and to reflect before we choose how we need to respond. This means we must allow time, space and grace to ask for and receive assistance. My dream and yours deserve no interruption. It deserves our complete focus and attention. By staying present in the moment, connected to our truth and inner knowing, and surrounded by people who support and elevate us, we can become a vibrational match for what we are ready to create, knowing we can rely on the Divine to provide help along the way.

It's critically important to me to make the people I connect with feel seen, heard, appreciated, and valued. I was asked if I was given one superpower, what would it be? I thought it might be cool to have knowledge of catastrophes in advance, so that I could prevent or avert them. Upon further thought, I changed my answer and decided that if I could truly be granted the gift of one superpower, I would choose to heal the world - one heart, mind, body and soul at a time. And then I realized that's what I've always done in my career, following my passion, listening to my intuition, leading with my heart. I have always been the person who has been a force for transformation in the lives of the people I come into contact with. One of the best compliments I've ever been given was when I asked a client of mine for feedback about what it is I do and they said, "you make everyone around you a better person."

I believe in the existing full untapped potential of each individual person. I believe in the possibility of human healing for all. I believe each of us need to step into the unique role only we were born to fill, our destiny, living our own best life. When we're each performing at our highest potential, we're also showing up in service to others. When we're aligned within our own masculine and feminine, we can truly give and receive. We can hold space, and fill it with color and emotion. We can be aligned within ourselves and be in alignment with the universe. It's not enough to sit quietly in a corner hiding our wisdom, talent, and power when it could be used to help others. As Gina DeVee says, "It's for such a time as this that I have been called."

THE IMPACT I AM READY TO CREATE IN THE WORLD

What does it mean to have an impact? There are many ways to have an impact on individuals, groups, society, the world as a whole, and the collective consciousness. I believe that one person with love, kindness, and an inner spark can set off a chain reaction, a revolution, and change the world. My weapon of choice is love. I think that you have the choice to rewrite your past and write your future story in such a way as to create a positive impact on others. As Brene Brown says, "Story speaks to our true language of emotion." Emotions help us understand, connect, and communicate with others as well as with ourselves. Feeling our emotions is important for survival and when felt fully, can help us live a more connected and full life.

It's time for me to make my contribution to the people that I can serve. I'm meant to be more than I have been to this point. Unfortunately, the busyness and traumas of life made me lose contact with my truth. I didn't see all the possibilities and opportunities in front of me. When you get clear on who you are, what you stand for, and what you were called here to do, it makes you brave and bold enough to express your desires and fight for them. I can't let the untruths of I don't have enough time, money, or knowledge stop me. I won't let the thoughts of why me, or the self-doubt or fears make me falter. Because in reality, we're not afraid of anything. Love is greater than fear. We need to love ourselves enough to fight for the truth and fight for our dreams.

We need to embrace with love the ideas and intuition that come to us, to accept the truth of our inner knowing, to ask for and accept with grace the guidance and help we require. I need to remind myself that I'm capable and the exact human to complete my dream. It's meant to be. It's meant for me. No matter what else calls me or requires my attention, I will not lose contact with my dreams. Now that I've reconnected with my inner knowing in the certainty of the Divine, it's time for me to realize my dreams. In fighting for my dreams and making them come to life, I can empower others to make their dreams come true as well.

We give others permission by living by example. Dreams need to be realized. Passions need to be fueled. When you create an impact on others it will energize you and allow you to create even more. Once you see the impact you can have on others, you will stop blocking yourself. Our own wounds can be healed by helping others. Be present and visible to people who want the same growth that you did. As I achieve my goals, I receive the double blessing of abundance and get to deliver all that I can to those I help and serve.

It's time for me to take a stand and use my voice for the greater good, to establish myself as a change maker, a disruptive force for healing and transformation. By sharing my story, and encouraging others to tell their stories, I can create greater human connection and shift the world. I've learned to be fully present with myself, to allow divine direction to inspire and motivate me to speak up for change through the power of human connection, relationships, and the collective.

ABOUT THE AUTHOR

DR. KRISTINA TICKLER WELSOME

Dr. Kristina Tickler Welsome is a Doctor of Physical Therapy, Owner of The Key To Wellness and The Key Publishing, a Holistic Life Transformation Coach and International Bestselling Author. Decades of professional experience with patients, students and clients makes her coaching effective, efficient and easily integrated into your life. Her passion is to support the well-being and healing of your heart, mind, body and soul as you learn to love your authentic self. Tina will empower you to become the author of your own life story, remove barriers to success and unlock your full potential to live a life you love. Her own personal life journey provided her with awareness, experience, knowledge and skills that shaped her into a newer version of herself. A more complete and integrated self who is ready to use her voice to amplify the voices of others to create even more impact in the world.

Website: www.thekeytowellness.net

18

ABOUT THE PUBLISHER

Inspired World Publishing was founded by former journalist Dina Behrman. It publishes solo and multi-author books from entrepreneurs, changemakers and business leaders with a story to tell and expertise to impart.

Publisher and PR strategist Dina Behrman works with entrepreneurs who want to take their business to the next level. She helps them to become a bestselling author and get featured in the press so they can stop being the internet's best kept secret, become the 'go to' expert and create an even bigger impact in the world.

She launched her business following a decade working as a journalist, during which she was published in virtually every national UK newspaper and many magazines. She's worked as a publicist for a number of 7-figure business owners, and has also helped hundreds of entrepreneurs learn how to do their own PR and get featured in the press globally. She's been featured in Forbes, Entrepreneur, Huff Post, The Guardian, BBC radio, amongst others.

To join her next multi-author book or find out more about her PR services visit www.dinabehrman.com.

"Small gestures can have a big impact. Create where it matters."

— JULIANNA MARGULIES

"In every day, there are 1,440 minutes. That means we have 1,440 daily opportunities to make a positive impact."

— LES BROWN

"Genius is in the idea. Impact, however, comes from action."

— SIMON SINEK

“Success is not measured in the amount of dollars you make, but the amount of lives you impact.”

— LEWIS HOWES

"Never underestimate the valuable and important difference you make in every life you touch. For the impact you make today has a powerful rippling effect on every tomorrow."

— LEON BROWN

"A life is not important except in the impact it has on other lives."

— JACKIE ROBINSON

"The only limit to your impact is your imagination and commitment."

— TONY ROBBINS

"Every action we take impacts the lives of others around us."

— ARTHUR CARMAZZI

"Recognise that every interaction you have is an opportunity to make a positive impact on others."

— SHEP HYKEN

"Most people are playing the game of compounding interest, which is self interest - how do they take care of themselves and produce more for themselves, storing value for their own benefit. I play a different game. A game I call 'compounding impact.' How do you make a positive impact in the world?"

— BROCK PIERCE